PRAYER, I

MW01171365

LEARNING TO HEAR GOD THROUGH PRAYER, DREAMS AND VISIONS

BY JEFF R. COWGILL

Num 12:6: "Hear now My words: If there is a prophet among you, I, the LORD, make Myself known to him in a vision; I speak to him in a dream.

Dedications

This book is dedicated to all the faithful men and women of God that inspired me in my journey.

An ancient rabbi when asked "What is God's purpose for our lives?" He responded, "To become more".

Our Pastors, Teachers, Mentors, and Friends who hold us up daily in prayer.

To my Children who don't know it yet but are going to find themselves reading this book and seeking God for wisdom and understanding for themselves and my Great Grandchildren.

And my wonderful wife Teresa who inspired me to keep working toward my goals, seeking the Lord for my family and for our Children.

Whom we will always cherish, no matter the failures in our lives or theirs. Even when they grow up and move out of our lives, we continue to hold them in prayer, and have hopes and dreams that they too will experience God's blessing on their lives and children.

And for our families who know who they are that continued to believe that there is more to us than meets the eye, I give thanks. I also want to thank those mighty prophets of God who spoke into our lives to endure, and saw promises of God around us, and most of all to God, who continues to richly bless us daily.

To my Mom and Pop who I love dearly, and my little brother Mark.

My idea is to take the wisdom I received from my communications with God and to impart it to you, not just with my interpretation, but with a Hebraic understanding about prayer, dreams, and visions.

I do understand that God's will is for us to become inaugurated with the blood of Christ as with the first blood covenant. As we also enter the new covenant with the blood of Jesus applied, I will introduce you to a way of meditating on God's debar (Word) or (Ark).

In this book I introduce meanings translated from our understanding of certain biblical terms and words and transliterate them into a whole new way of perceiving concepts and ideologies from the Hebrew language.

Some sages and rabbi's believe that a lot of the meanings have been lost in translation, and I too have come to realize that God's meanings for certain passages have been lost. Let us investigate the light of God's Word together for understanding that may enlighten our paths.

Shalom Blessings

Forward

Dreams are typical; everyone has them, even animals. So, what do they mean is the common question? Throughout the books of the Bible and from the beginning of time the ancients desired to know what they mean and just what dreams really are. Are they more than just wandering thoughts, last night's pizza, or something much more? Are they promises that come to men and women from God, not only to guide them, but alter the very course of history.

Time after time references to dreams and interpretation bring prosperity and dominion to the men and women of the Bible.

Jacob left Beersheba and went to Haran. The sun had already set when he came to a good place to spend the night. He took a rock there and laid his head on it to sleep. He had a dream there was a ladder that was on the ground and reached up into heaven. He saw the angels of God going up and down the ladder.

And then Jacob saw the Lord standing by the ladder. He said, "I am the God of your grandfather Abraham. I am the God of Isaac.

I will give you the land that you are lying on now. I will give this land to you and to your children. You will have as many descendants as there are particles of dust on the earth. They will spread east and west, north and south.
All the families on earth will be blessed because of you and your descendants. "I am with you, and I will protect you everywhere you go. I will bring you back to this land. I will not leave you until I have done what I have promised."

Then Jacob woke up and said, "I know that the Lord is in this place, but I did not know he was here until I slept."

Jacob was afraid and said, "This is a very great place. This is the house of God. This is the gate to heaven." So Jacob named it Bethel.

He is provoked to follow God and receive his inheritance among his people because of this dream.

His son Joseph had a dream, and when he told it to his brothers, they hated him all the more. He said to them, "Listen to this dream I had: We were binding sheaves of grain out in the field when suddenly my sheaf rose and stood upright, while your sheaves gathered around mine and bowed down to it."

His brothers said to him, "do you intend to reign over us? They became jealous and sought to kill him, however sold him into slavery in Egypt. He ultimately interprets Pharaoh's dream and with this comes promotion and blessing for his entire generation.

When Solomon went up to Gibeon the high place to sacrifice, while he was sleeping the Lord came to him in a vision of the night and the Lord asked what he desired, (1 Kings 3) and he asked of the Lord for an understanding heart to discern between good and evil. When he woke up, he realized it had been a dream, but the Lord gave him wealth and riches, and honor besides wisdom and knowledge.

This book looks into the truth about what dreams are, why we should pay attention to small details, and how we can use dreams to promote our prayer life.

In my own experiences dreams can become the catalyst that bring us into a closer relationship with God. Can we allow the Holy Spirit to intercede with us even while our natural mind is at rest?

In a dream, in a vision of the night, When deep sleep falleth upon men, In slumberings upon the bed; Then he openeth the ears of men, And sealeth their instruction, That he may withdraw man from his purpose, And hide pride from man. He keepeth back his soul from the pit, And his life from perishing by the sword. Job 33:15

For it is the spirit of man say's the Lord, I will search the reigns of Men's hearts while they sleep, while they slumber upon their beds. Can God bypass the intellect of men and deal directly with the thoughts and intents of the heart? Can He test the reigns of men's hearts and determine if he is ready for promotion?

There is testing that goes along with asking God for purpose. When God gives a man a vision, He is saying to him, now what will you do? Will you write the vision, will you run with it? Habakkuk 2:2

Ask yourself, is my mind on the foolish things of this world, or do I meditate on things that could increase my wisdom and understanding of God's word?

The word meditate means:

- meditate הֲגוֹתל_
Pronounce, utter, meditate, articulate, vocalize, and murmur

An experience I had back in 2011 around the time of Yom Kippur (Day of Atonement, 10th day of the seventh month, Holy Convocation, To Cover, can also be found in the original Hebrew name for the Mercy Seat of the Ark of the Covenant which in the Hebrew bible is called "Kaporet" meaning covering.

Prayer:

As I made my way into the throne room, the Lord say's, I have asked you many times to go to your neighbor and repent, but you have not obeyed my voice. I had some issues beforehand which I won't go into at this point, but it was not laid to rest.

So, I rose up and went, and before I could even reach my destination, I began to weep under the anointing and power of God. The neighbor that I needed to ask to forgive me reached out to me and we made peace.

When I returned to the Lord, there was such a powerful presence in the atmosphere. He took me to the laver, a mirror in my case and showed me the condition of my inner man. I asked God to forgive me and change my life and that's when I began to have powerful dreams and visions.

On November 07, 2011 I received an impartation and visitation from the Lord that changed my life. It made my desire to seek Him not only in prayer life, but meditation on the word, and in my sleeping time as well. I remember waking up with my hands lifted into the air praising God and speaking in another tongue.

In another session I woke up reciting scriptures from Numbers, line by line, precept upon precept, and when I got up to go to the restroom, I heard the Holy Spirit say "am I going to fast". These occurrences are not uncommon when you become in love with God's word, and it becomes a part of you.

For the first time in my life, I could honestly say, I and my father are one!

Just think if a person lives to be 60 years old, 20 years of that will be spent sleeping, it only seems logical to ask God to speak to us in dreams and visions.

7

When I go to bed at night, I pray, Oh Lord, speak to me through the Holy Spirit while I sleep, search the reigns of my heart Oh Lord, minister to me that I might be given something to increase me.

After all it is God's plan for us to become more, to become the potential of His plans for us.

It is written in Jeremiah 29:11, for I know the plans I have for you," says the LORD. "They are plans for good and not for disaster, to give you a future and a hope."

We can look into these dreams with a little humor, some degree of curiosity, but hopefully a newfound respect for our dreams, what they mean, and why God uses them to communicate to his people. It's all in how we learn to respect and seek after a word of wisdom or enlightenment.

We can find knowledge through many forms, such as it has been written in Psalms 8:2, Matthew 21:16, out of the mouth of babes.

Did you ever have "De jav ue" when you knew you had been somewhere before or you were in the process of doing something that at one time or another you have already done? Dreams have a way of showing up in our waking lives, could it be a prompt for us to fulfill a purpose?

These are questions we will try and find some reasonable understanding for age old questions as we search and study the scriptures in this book. I probably won't be able to answer all your questions; however, I intend to show that knowledge and wisdom are given to those who seek the face of God.

If it comes through prayer, visions, or dreams, its knowledge that you did not have or study in a book, but it just came through revelation of a higher order.

These next chapters deal with understanding imparted from various resources, including a deep relationship with our God. Soon you will find some answers to help in your quest for a dynamic relationship with Jesus Christ.

We will find it's the intimacy of knowing Him that brings supernatural wisdom and understanding.

In these next few chapters you will find types of dreams, visions and revelation from personal experiences and encounters from a prayerful perspective.

Thanks for taking the time to read and help me to appreciate the wisdom of God!

Contents

Chapter 1 Alef – Impartation through a dream

Through these writings I have used references and scientific documents to show my cause and effect, through theological, metaphysical, scientific and spiritual means so to better elaborate between dreams, visions, and experiences of physical and dream phenomena.

Phenomena: an object or aspect known through the senses rather than by thought or intuition.

I would like to emphasize and can't express in any certain terms the importance of God given dreams that encourage us to seek God, know God, and love God. Our dreams are given to correct us, draw us, excite us, warn us, exhort us and teach us.

One type of dream is a <u>correction dream</u>. These types of dreams might come in an answer to a prayer or just a rebuke by the Holy Spirit to bring repentance into our lives.

He that the Father loves He chastened, and scourges every son whom he receives. KJV HEB 12:6

Correction dream:

An example of a correction dream I had is entered below;

Date: 02/04/2012
Title: Smoking church
Type: Correction
Dream Text: In this dream I was in a small church praying for some children, and then I noticed everyone had returned to their seats. As I began to look around, I noticed everyone was lighting and smoking cigarettes. I saw the man next to me and I said, "That's not a very good example", then he said, "What's wrong with smoking"? And I looked him right in the eye and said "Sir! Do you even own a Bible"?
Then while I was looking at everyone else, he put his cigarette out on my hand, right on the back of it. Well, I must interject here that it felt real. (Sometimes when I testify of this event, I have been known to develop a stigmata. A stigmata is a holy sign given to verify the authenticity of an experience with God to bring revelation and build faith to the witnesses. (see Transfiguration details later in this book).

I jumped up and went to hit him right in the face, when he threw up his arm and blocked me, then I went to hit him again when suddenly, there was a tap on my shoulder. I knew who it was even without looking, and the Lord said look and pointed to the pulpit. As I looked toward the front of the church, there was an ashtray on the pulpit and the preacher had a cigar and sideburns. It was me!

I had been such a hypocrite I couldn't even see; I had once myself been a bad example. I shouldn't judge people because I once walked in their shoes. Do you believe that God would visit me and correct me for wrong thinking or a proud heart?

Biblical examples of dream prophetic:

In the book of (Matthew 1:20; 2:13): Joseph would have divorced Mary when he found out she was pregnant, but God sent an angel to him in a dream, convincing him that the pregnancy was of God. Joseph went ahead with the marriage. After Jesus was born, God sent two more dreams, one to tell Joseph to take his family to Egypt so Herod could not kill Jesus, and another to tell him Herod was dead and that he could return home.

In the book of (Acts 10:9-15): While Peter was praying at the 4th hour on the rooftop of a house in Joppa, God gave him a vision of animals lowered in something like a sheet. A voice from heaven told Peter to kill the animals (some of which were unclean) and eat them. The vision served to show that Christians are not bound by kosher law and that God had pronounced Gentiles "clean"; that is, heaven is open to all who follow Jesus.

The secular side of dreams exhorts us to righteousness, on the Biblical side we know that God is our righteousness and only He can lead us to righteousness. Dreams can be used for self-correction, awareness of faults, or allow our consciences to convict us.

There was a king named Abimelek who God gave a correction dream which in the dream God said "thou art a dead man, for thou hast took another man's wife.

Genesis 20:3 who took Abraham's wife Sarah to wife. He had no prior knowledge before the dream that Sarah was not the sister, but the wife of Abraham. We established the knowledge came through the dream.
In these writings my intent is to show that unknown knowledge can come through dreams.

Dreams are one of the most overlooked forms of communication used by God.

The Word of God consistently reveals God as speaking to people through this universally experienced and mysterious phenomenon. The Lord uses dreams for a variety of purposes:

*- to warn global leaders of future events. (**Gen. 41:1-8**)*
*- to provide revelation to His prophets (**Num. 12:6**)*
*- to warn us against certain decisions. (**Matt. 27:17-19**)*
*- to reveal His divine destiny for our lives. (**Gen. 37:5-8**)*
*- to answer our recent petitions and prayers. (**I Kings 3:5-15**)*

It is important to realize that dreams could be more if we choose them to be, we can ask God to intervene in our lives, to communicate with us on a higher plane, to bypass the intellect of our minds, and commune with our hearts. Our hearts do not lie to God. When he tests the reigns of your heart, he is corresponding to your true nature. It's the spirit within a man who God contends with. Throughout the history God's only desire was to have a relationship with men and women.
He became the living Menorah or lampstand, the Ark of the Covenant in the Torah, the Mishkan (Tent of Meeting), then manifested as a human being in John 1:14 to dwell with his creation.

In Hebrew text the heart was used in place of mind or thought. Speaking of what is the intent of the heart rather than a changed mind. The relationship with God, or rather loving God will cause our thoughts to change. It is important to clarify here that if you have a dream and feel that perhaps God gave it to you, prayerfully examine the Word of God and make sure your dream is in agreement with Scripture.

If it is, prayerfully consider what God would have you do in response to your dream (James 1:5). In Scripture, whenever anyone experienced a dream from God, God always made the meaning of the dream clear, *whether directly to the person, through an angel, or through another messenger **(Genesis 40:5–11; Daniel 2:45; 4:19)**. When God speaks to us, He makes sure His message is clearly understood.*

Dreams are a phenomenon He created within us, to speak to us to alert us to danger we've been ignoring, to convict us of sin, to remind us of obligations, or sharpen our focus on problems we've been trying to suppress. The conscious and sub-conscious are the same candle as in Proverbs 25, the candle before the Lord.

How does God build your faith? The first thing God does to build your faith is give you a dream. When God wants to work in your life, he'll always give you a dream—about yourself, about what he wants you to do, about how he's going to use your life to impact the world.

There are many examples in the Bible of this.

- *God gave Noah the dream of building an ark.*

- *God gave Abraham the dream of being the father of a great nation.*

- *God gave Joseph the dream of being a leader that would save his people.*

- *God gave Nehemiah the dream of building the wall around Jerusalem.*

An example of a Prophetic dream I had entered below

Date: 05/19/2015
Title: Pillar
Type: Prophetic Prophecy

I was setting across the table from a red haired man. I noticed the table was very large and directly behind him were some very large pillars of stone. I was weeping while the man began to ask me to trust him, that if I did, he would not let me down. Then I heard the words "red hair in power". I wanted to tell the man what the pillars represented in the dream.

I searched the Word of God for occurrences of a pillar and found Revelations 3:12

I will make him a pillar in the temple of my God. Never shall he go out of it, and I will write on him the name of my God, and the name of the city of my God, the new Jerusalem, which comes down from my God out of heaven, and my own new name. Rev 3:12 KJV

<u>Pillar</u> *- means strength and support, also a reference for name of God.*

<u>Red hair</u> *- means wisdom and anointing.*

In my journal I drew a great pillar or column which used to be used to hold up great buildings.

During the actual inauguration of President Trump at the Lincoln center, I saw President Trump sitting behind the exact table with the stone pillars I saw in my vision.

I believe I was seeing the actual inauguration of President Trump in the vision. In 2015 Trump formally announced his candidacy for president June 16th in New York.

How do you know when a dream is from God or when it's just something you've thought up yourself? The Bible tells us that God, "by his mighty power at work within us is able to do far more than we would ever dare to ask or even dream of—infinitely beyond our highest prayers, desires, thoughts, or hopes." (Ephesians 3:20 LB)

In other words, if a dream comes from God, it will be so big in your life that you can't do it on your own. If you could do it on your own, you wouldn't need faith. And if you don't have faith you're not pleasing God, because the Bible says whatever is not of faith is sin. (Roman 14:23) God starts to build your faith by giving you a dream. He may be speaking to you now, but you just don't recognize it for what it is. That dream you have—the idea, the concept —that thing you've been thinking about doing that would be of real benefit to other people, where do you think that idea came from?

God will never tell you to do something that contradicts his truth. In other words, he won't give you a dream of leaving your family and kids and moving to Hollywood to be a movie star. If you've got that dream, then you can know it is not from God.

God starts with a dream as he works within your life to build faith.

In this next text we will delve into the history of dream analysis so we can better understand both spiritual and metaphysical applications.

The History of Dream Analysis

No one knows the true origins of dream analysis, or how long it has been going on. Chances are, however, that the analysis and interpretation of dreams, in some fashion, has been taking place almost as long as people have been dreaming.

Dreams must have been both fascinating and terrifying to our ancient ancestors, and they were most likely very confused by this strange form of consciousness. We do know that many ancient civilizations placed great importance on the situations encountered in their dreams, and used those situations to cast light on their waking lives.

As a matter of fact, many civilizations did not see a distinction between the waking world and the world of dreams, but instead saw one as merely an extension of the other.

Of course dream analysis and dream interpretation is still in use today, and it has been used successfully to deal with all manner of traumas and emotional issues. For instance, it is known that those suffering from Post-Traumatic Stress Disorder (PTSD), are often troubled by nightmares.

Dealing with the underlying cause of the PTSD, through a combination of therapies and psychological techniques, can banish those nightmares as well.

In dream journaling I suggest to acknowledge a dream by writing it down. Then with prayer and the gift of discernment either dismiss it as what it is, or accept it as truth or a lie of the enemy. If we agree with it, it becomes truth. The power of life and death are in the power of the tongue, or confession.

Some of the earliest references to dreams and their interpretation occurs in the Bible, and the Bible is full of references to the dreams of prophets and other notable people.

The ancient Greek and Roman world was also full of dream interpreters and analysis, and the Greek and Roman government and military alike used the services of professional dream interpreters to determine the best course of political action and even the best strategy for battle.

Dream interpreters were even taken along as troops prepared for battle, and their prognostications were taken very seriously, as were the dreams of the generals and the troops.

In the ancient world, the Greek philosopher Aristotle was a big propend of dream interpretation, and he spoke about the illusion of the senses that allowed dreams to occur. He later came to believe that disturbances of the body were the cause of dreams.

Many ancient peoples thought that dreams were a way for the soul to commune with the spirit world. In many cultures, the soul was thought to leave the body at night, and dreams were thought of as a way of communicating with, and gaining information about, departed relatives and ancient ancestors alike.

Even today, many people place great significance on dreams and dreaming, and many people continue to see a spiritual element in the dream world. Dreams still remain largely a mystery to science, and this mystery has helped to spur thoughts that dreams contain more than a mere physical meaning.

Dream interpretation continues to be used, both as a fun hobby and as a serious scientific pursuit. Dream research is one of the most fascinating, and widely studied, elements of psychological research, and new dream studies continue to reveal hidden insights about the world of dreams.

New symbols, too, continue to emerge from the world of dream analysis and dream research. From Carl Jung to Sigmund Freud to modern psychologists and psychiatrists, many people have strived, and continue to strive, to understand the hidden meanings, and hidden messages, of our dreams.

There are many dream types which we have to consider while analyzing our dreams. The first and most important thing that I've discovered is to first ask yourself, is my dream from God? How do we determine if it is from God or a as Ira Millington say's in his book "Understanding the dream you dream an incoherent dream or rambling".

When we learn to communicate with God by speaking to Him in prayer and hearing His voice, he might often answer our questions when we are not even thinking about what we have asked.

John 14:26
But the comforter, which is the Holy Ghost, whom the Father will send in My name, He shall teach you all things, and bring all things to your remembrance, whatsoever I have said unto you.

Even if your dream is not from God, we should value it and write it down for future reference. Sometimes the dreams that we discerned were not from God, ultimately we find there was some lesson to be had even if we dismiss the dream as a soulish dream.

It is our spirit that truly knows us, not our conscious mind (Cor. 2:11). Our spirits may try to cry out for help to us in the night, these messages can be understood using the same method and keys used with other dreams. Since some of our dreams are not from God, we should exercise reasonable caution when we apply them.

Then we can determine if it meets the criteria so that it may be used as viable information for our walk with God.

There are both secular and spiritual means for diagnosing dream characteristics, here are some secular types as follows:

Ordinary, Anxiety, Fragment, Lucid, Nightmare, Telepathic, Prophetic, Premonitory, Daydream, Initial, Wish fulfillment, Sleep paralysis, Erotic, Numinous, Layered, and Recurring.

Since we are looking at the spiritual concept of communication in dreams and visions we won't delve into this platform, but I want to emphasize the knowledge of it for the sake of relevance.

I have studied many theories based on these methods. Sigmund Freud studied subjects and determined that the mind was capable of producing all types of anomalies'.

The Spiritual diagnostic of a dream does apply its basis from scripture however and most Christians try to compare everything based on this guide.
Another mentor and teacher of mine who came on the scene in the 1980's 90's and has recently been on the Christian T.V. Stations is John Paul Jackson of Streams Ministries. John teaches the Biblical aspect of interpretation of dreams and applies it to logistics and simplistic. If you have a dream that the Lord say's don't eat Chocolate and you're a diabetic, then what is the Lord saying? Some of the types of dream categories we use are:

Prophetic or Revelation – Provides insight of knowledge that you did not have prior to the dream, or gives a deeper understanding based on its content.

Calling or Conformation – Dreams that provide comfort or conformation of a specific call, duty or assignment from God. Sometimes could be in the form of a messenger or angelic being.

Courage – An Exhortation to bravery or to pursue something you think is above your power.

Direction – Usually to confirm a behavior or movement towards something.

Invention – Guidelines or pictures, instructions to create.

Word of Knowledge – Information that one did not have prior to the dream or vision. (Always make sure it lines up with scripture).

Correction – Usually a unique way of chastisement by the Lord in a way that is received by the dreamer. Only God knows how best to correct his children.

Warning – God sent a dream to Laban, in Genesis 31 to warn him not to good or bad to Jacob when he caught him after fleeing from him. God sent a dream to Abimelek and said "thou art a dead man, for thou hast took another man's wife. Genesis 20:3

Self-Condition – a look into our true nature, who we are. God sometimes shows our own condition through a circumstance or situation.

Healing – God sometimes can reach to our spirits and perform a unique miracle.

Deliverance – a prayer of salvation or freedom from habits or sickness.

Flushing – When we have a dream where we have been exposed to people or places that our spirit needs to dispose of.

Dark – Dreams that take us into place that are terrifying.

False Dreams – Dreams that we discern as not true.

Fear Dreams – Dreams that torment or make us fearful.

Spiritual Warfare – Dreams were we are fighting an evil force.

Intercession – Dreams were we are praying for those who are sick or need deliverance.

Chemical – Dreams that are triggered by chemicals released from our bodies.

Body Dreams – Dreams that are initiated from a tired soul or a desire of the natural.

Though, as you began to develop through the keeping of your dreams, you will discover that while praying and seeking Him in your waking life God begins to deal with you spiritually. (Job 33:15) indicates that while a man sleeps and slumbers upon his bed, God communes with man's spirit, searches the reigns of the heart. God may put you in a certain situation to see how you respond to it.

These dreams start off with dreams that have not been classified using dream analysis or any types of modern dream interpretation methods, but as we progress you will discover that the dreams began to take a different format. I begin to use a format called dream analysis which allows the dreamer to section off the dream and look for symbols, or meaning embedded into the dream.

We began to break down the dream using this process to better define the dream, to determine if it has any basis, or intellectual meaning to the dreamer. We look at backdrop, objects, colors, places, feelings, or people to determine what this may mean in our waking lives.

God communicates through a variety of ways including dreams and visions.

In fact about one third of the Bible deals with some kind of visionary experience. Much of the details within Eschatology (the study of the end times) are based on the dreams and visions of people like Daniel and John. Without those visionary experiences we would be largely in the dark concerning the culmination of this age.

In this study we will largely look at dreams. The Bible identifies dreams as visions of the night (Job 33:15)

Definitions:

Dream: "A sequence of images etc. passing through a sleeping person's mind" (Webster's Dictionary)

Vision: "A mental image" (Webster's Dictionary)

Importance and validity of visionary experience

Visionary experiences are valid, scriptural ways for God to communicate to man. Modern western society's way of gaining knowledge and understanding rests upon reason and logic. They largely refuse to recognize the validity of visionary experiences because these do not often fall within the realm of logical reasoning. It is interesting to note that the Bible does not warn us against dreams and visions. In fact instead of a negative stance towards visionary experience, the Bible is surprisingly positive concerning dreams and visions. Let me share but a few verses. There are many more examples:

Num 12:6: "Hear now My words: If there is a prophet among you, I, the LORD, make Myself known to him in a vision; I speak to him in a dream.

Hos 12:10: I have also spoken by the prophets, and have multiplied visions; I have given symbols through the witness of the prophets."

Ps 16:7: I will bless the LORD who has given me counsel; my heart also instructs me in the night seasons.

Job 33:14-18: For God may speak in one way, or in another, yet man does not perceive it. In a dream, in a vision of the night, when deep sleep falls upon men, while slumbering on their beds, Then He opens the ears of men, and seals their instruction. In order to turn man from his deed, and conceal pride from man, He keeps back his soul from the Pit, and his life from perishing by the sword.

Dan. 2:30: But as for me, this secret has not been revealed to me because I have more wisdom than anyone living, but for our sakes who make known the interpretation to the king, and that you may know the thoughts of your heart.

Acts 2:17: And it shall come to pass in the last days, says God,

That I will pour out of My Spirit on all flesh; your sons and your daughters shall prophesy, your young men shall see visions, your old men shall dream dreams.

As we can see dreams have made quite an impact on us through the history of mankind. If there is another reason for us to dream I couldn't think of any better reasons, unless it's to provide us with correction and chastisement from our Lord.

As we see in the next chapters how God can speak to us for our good. Let us learn to keep open the communications so that we may be able to receive revelation and understanding from our God.

Language of visionary experience

Visionary experiences are communicated in a distinct language of pictures and symbols. This language is not written in paragraphs, it is painted in pictures on the canvass of the heart or projected on the screen of the spirit.

This language has its own vocabulary in the form of symbols. The Lord seals the instruction of your heart in the night seasons. If you understand the symbols and pictures flowing from your heart, you'll be able to interpret what your dreams mean.

Habakkuk said: I will [in my thinking] stand upon my post of observation and station myself on the tower or fortress, and will watch to see what He will say within me. . . (Hab. 2:1 AMP) Here he is looking and not just listening. He is focused to see the symbols or pictures within him painted by the Lord in his spirit.

I was speaking with my wife this weekend and it seems that sometimes our revelations come from just sharing God's Word with each other, or rather breaking bread.

In this I mean as we begin to share our experiences with each other kind of like a pot luck at church, where some might bring spinach, some rice, some chicken, what is good to you may not appeal to some. But, as we begin to share a dream, or impartation it takes shape, and becomes clear even to the speaker or revealer of the impartation.
I for one have been telling a dream to an individual as the Holy Spirit impressed me to share, and as I was sharing the substance it seem to come alive, and I realized my understanding was magnified. The dream was for a word of knowledge for the person whom I was ministering. It was a key that was fashioned for the individual, and God knew I would soon cross their path. I was being prepared for the encounter with knowledge for the future that I did not have prior to the dream.

I heard John Paul Jackson (American Author, teacher, conference speaker, prophet and founder of Streams Ministries) say, that a dream might not be given for interpretation of the future, but for future interpretation.

It is my belief that God has a way to speak to each individual in a unique way with signs that only you can get the true meaning. Because he truly knows your heart and how to communicate with you as He made you! It may be true we can use some generic references to unite our understanding, but with a true vision, only we can truly understand what God is relaying to us.

John Paul Jackson's interpretation charts are helpful in getting an idea of what we might be seeing, and is good for a guide because it relates to a biblical perspective, unlike the more secular interpretations such as Sigmund Freud, or gnostic scientific dream analysis methods.

It is my belief after many books and studies pertaining to dreams, visions, and impartations that sometimes God may use symbols or even people to point us in certain directions, sort of like beacons to get us on the right path or destination.

Many times reading I have read where prophets received direction from a person whom they admired, or knew personally, or maybe just a faceless deity or angel of the Lord. It doesn't really matter as long as we take it for what it is. Usually in the simplest form possible we can learn from these experiences.

In the book Seer by James Goll, (American Author, director of Prayer Storm, Coordinator of Encounters Alliance), he explains experiences of people who received impartation and encouragement from those who had passed on. They could be a relative, or someone they knew from the past who had a gift or an acknowledgement to encourage.

Usually I have found it most often to be an encouragement and exhortation to help them through a tough time or season of life's change. In recent experiences it could also to pass down a mantle or gift.

I was having this conversation with my wife and told her about the visit from Sir Isaac Newton. She simply stated maybe he is passing down a mantle. Wow, I thought, how did this not occur to me before, a mantle or blessing from those who have become saints before us?

The Bible speaks in Ephesians 6 that we should pray for the saints to persevere. This means that we are to be supportive of one another, it also say's all saints. Some may not even be alive anymore, but it never say's that they cannot pray and encourage us within limits.

Let's take a look at the transfiguration of Jesus, there he was visited by Moses and Elijah.
The word "transfiguration" comes from the Latin roots Trans- ("across") and figure ("form, shape"). It thus signifies a change of form or appearance.

Angels, Messengers can appear during trying times to encourage, exhort and impart to us as needed, when we pray, God can send help just as Daniel prayed and God had send an Angel to help as in Daniel 10 12,14.

This is what happened to Jesus in the event known as the Transfiguration: His appearance changed and became glorious. The Transfiguration was a special event in which God allowed certain apostles to have a privileged spiritual experience that was meant to strengthen their faith for the challenges they would later endure.

But it was only a temporary event. It was not meant to be permanent. In the same way, at certain times in this life, God may give certain members of the faithful (not all of the faithful, all the time), special experiences of his grace that strengthen their faith.

A sign or symbol does not mean the same to everyone all the time, as we grow, mature and time moves on the seasons come and go, fashions change, technology changes however God still speaks.

The Word of God tells us that if we seek His face first, early that he will prepare our way that our foot shall not stumble in darkness, that he shall be the light of our path.

Understanding the principles of who God is: Why He can and will impart to us. It's God's nature to restore, create, and love us.

Before God spoke out of himself, He is Aleph, singular, masculine, all by himself, Echad or One, so where did the Word reside? In himself?

The created language or speech and breath which proceeded out of God was and is God and a "Thing, Dabar, Word, or Ark, a covering or container (tent) to reside outside of God, so it became beit the Hebrew second beside himself, behold the Word of God.

The Word is the created image of God of Himself. That is created of God is God.

John 1 (Yochanan 1)

In the beginning was the Word, and the Word was with God, and the Word was God. He was with God in the beginning.
All things came to be through him, and without him nothing made had being. In him was life, and the life was the light of mankind. The light shines in the darkness, and the darkness has not suppressed it.

John (Yockanan 14)

The Word became a human being and lived with us and we saw his Sh'khinah, the Sh'khinah of the Fathers only Son, full of grace and truth.

Bet is the second number in the Hebrew alphabet and means a tent or container that something is stored in, or covering. Bethlehem was also the place where our Lord was established on earth, the place literally means "House of Bread", in Arabic "House of Meat".

According to the Hebrew bible the tabernacle (mishkan) meaning residence or dwelling place known as the Tent of the Congregation, also known as the Tent of Meeting was the portable earthly dwelling place of Yahweh (the God of Israel).

Exodus 33:14 God answered Moshe, set your mind at rest – my presence will go with you.

Exodus 25:8 "They are to make me a sanctuary, so that I may live among them"

John 1:14 And the Word was flesh or Human Being and lived among us.

Dwell from the greek skene derives from the Hebrew Mishkan, showing that in his incarnation Yeshua made his Tabernacle with his people. Thus, through Yeshua God did dwell with his people.

Revelation 21:1-6 It is done and he will live with them. They will be his people, and he himself, God with them, will be their God.

Jesus simply put became the Tent of Meeting or Living Earthly Tabernacle among his people. He became the Mercy Seat, Ark of the Covenant, and Our High Priest, a cohen gadol after the order of Malki-Tzedek.

Ex 33:7 the tent was outside the camp because of the Lord's estrangement from his people (Ex 33:3) following their making the golden calf. Jesus was crucified outside the gate because of His estrangement from his people. He has become and is the Tent of Meeting as we have to meet Him outside the gate at the cross before we can know Him as our savior. Then we can experience the pillar of cloud and the fire of the Ruach HaKodesh.

1 Cor. 6:19 explains that one's physical body is the tabernacle of the Spirit of God.

God existed outside of the container, outside of the physical parameters of time, space, and earth. Before time He is, Before Protons, Neutrons, Electrons, He is. God reached inside Himself and the Elohim, Masculine and singular, God is God All by Himself.

When God spoke outside of Himself it became an image or shape of Himself. Then it became more than one, it became Bet, a container or shape and image of HE Himself to dwell in, as a tent or house. The same word for thing is Ark or Word. The Hebrew word is Dabar meaning " "a word or the substance of a thing.

Midbar in Hebrew is derived from this word meaning, "Wilderness" or place where "God speaks". God speaks from the chaotic or chaos, bringing it to a halt.

(The number 3 in Hebrew is Gimel meaning a camel or foot, in other words a mode of transportation or transmission. It kind of makes sense there were three representing communication as this was meant to exhort the disciples and Jesus himself.

On the 3rd day God caused the dry land to appear conforming to what God said to it. He truly is Yahweh, interpreted as "He Who Makes That Which Has Been Made" or HE Brings into Existence Whatever Exist.

Yeshua, who is a forerunner through the parokhet (the curtain that covered the Ark of the Conenant), who has become a cohen gadol forever to be compared with Malki-Tzedek, the king of Shalem.

If the Aharon HaKodesh of the tribe of Levi had been enough to reach our goal, then there would not have been a need or necessity for transformation of Torah. For the system of cohanim is transformed, because our Lord arose out of Y'hudah and no one had served as priest from this tribe.

For we see that Yeshua is from another tribe and not by virtue of a rule in the Torah concerning physical descent, but by virtue of the power of an indestructible life.

Jesus was the House of God, (born in Beth-le-hem, meaning "House of Bread", in Arabic "House of Meat", the tabernacle in the flesh or container of God, One or Aleph the silent breath of God, Two or Bet , the Tent or Covering , spoken thing, metaphysical, or Word Container. Three or Gimel, transportation or importation of the Word of God toward us. Four Dalet or Door or Entry of to), See Rev 4(behold, I AM THE DOOR).

In this moment, God has ordained, and spoken over and fortified his word that if you receive what is being illuminated for you, you can obtain it and use this knowledge for the good.

After all the Word say's He knew you from your mother's womb, Jeremiah 1:5. Can we not think to say' if God knows me, then why would he not care for me, lead me through the turbulence of life.

When the container of God was crushed and <u>broken open in Gethsemane,</u> (Derived from two Hebrew words, gat, which means place of pressing, and shemani, which means oils of the anointing), also the Garden of Gethsemane, <u>the place of crushing</u>. Then on to Jerusalem to become the Lamb of God, (to break open, to become the repairer of the breach), or <u>bearer of sins</u> for the sacrifice of <u>Passover</u> (Pesach) in Hebrew.

Jesus stood before the people as Pilate asked, "Who shall I release to you today, Jesus of Nazareth or Barabbas? This is a picture of the hearts of those who had to choose who should be released. It wasn't that they loved Barabbas, but the hatred for truth that led the way.

Just as the priest would stand before the people with the two he goats and declare one to be sacrificed and one to set free, Jesus was to pay for the sins and Barabbas was to be set free that day. A shadow of Shavuot, just like on mount Sinai when the law of God was given to the children of Israel, now the Holy Ghost which comes in Jesus Name, or new Word covenant, after 50 days the Holy Spirit was poured out to all who would receive it in the upper room at Pentecost.

The Lord say's in dreams and visions in the last day's shall I speak to my people, your young men shall see visions and your old men shall dream dreams.

Having difficulties in life, well sometimes we might need to hear a word of chastisement from the Lord, or rebuke. It seems when God wants to speak it usually comes in a dream.

As in the smoking church dream, something I identified as being nasty or dirty is an ashtray. So God used that to illustrate to me that there may be something that is nasty or displeasing to in my life so He may show me what it is.

Let's say for example I may have made a remark or said something to someone that may have hurt their feelings. Later on I might have a dream, I might be reminded of what I said before the Lords presence, and then I might see the symbol of an ashtray. That would indicate to me that what I said was not pleasing or unclean.

I might have like Peter a prejudice God wants to unveil to me. As he did on the rooftop when Peter saw the four corners of the sheet let down with all manner of creeping things.

The Lord say's to Peter, what I have cleansed call not thou dirty. What, an open rebuke to Peter? Why would God do this? Because to make Peter's outcome better and to prepare him for his destiny. What Father will not discipline his children? Is the word disciple not derived from the word discipline?

We should welcome these experiences for the graces they are, but we should not expect them to continue indefinitely, nor should we be afraid or resentful when they cease.

They may have been meant only as momentary glimpses of the joy of heaven to sustain us as we face the challenges of this life, to help strengthen us on the road that will--ultimately--bring us into the infinite and endless joy of heaven. How much more would God seek to strengthen us to continue our journey steadfast?

On the mountain the three of them see the glory of God's Kingdom shining out of Jesus.

On the mountain they are overshadowed by God's holy cloud.

On the mountain—in the conversation of the transfigured Jesus with the Law and the Prophets—they realize that the true Feast of Tabernacles has come.

On the mountain they learn that Jesus himself is the living Torah, the complete Word of God.

On the mountain they see the 'power' (dynamis) of the Kingdom that is coming in Christ" (Jesus of Nazareth, vol. 1, p. 317).

Why did the Transfiguration take place? The Catechism explains it this way:
Christ's Transfiguration aims at strengthening the apostles' faith in anticipation of his Passion: the ascent onto the 'high mountain' prepares for the ascent to Calvary.
Christ, Head of the Church, manifests what his Body contains and radiates in the sacraments: 'the hope of glory'.

I have been encouraged in a lot of ways, through many preachers and men and women of God. As a prison Chaplain for many years I had the opportunity to meet many great men who were mighty in battle, taught me the Word of God and helped me through some rough times in my life.

Charles MaHaney (see below left) the great man of God who lead the United Pentecostal Church Prison Fellowship for many years imparted encouragement to me,(Book author He's My God Too) and I have to mention Rev. Bob McCool (below right) and his Grandson Billy McCool performing in the great state of Arkansas who I sat under for 24 years in the First United Pentecostal Church, who lead thousands to God.

Once I had a dream where I was sitting on the edge of a great stone window overlooking God's beauty, and I heard a voice behind me. I turned to look and it was Bro. and Sis. McCool Sr. and she was kindly asking me a question. She asked me "Jeff, when are you going to write your canticles"? I never even knew what a canticle was until this dream and don't remember hearing it before. After looking the word up I realized, it is basically my testimonies and admiration for the Lord.

Many times I thought, if I can just stumble into Gods presence with a pen and paper, I could write for hours upon hours. New revelation comes on a daily basis when you're seeking for it.

Chapter 3 – Gimel The Dragon and the Tongue

*The **Book of Revelation**, often called the **Revelation to John**, the **Apocalypse of John**, or simply **Revelation** or **Apocalypse**, is a book of the New Testament that occupies a central place in Christian Eschatology.*

Its title is derived from the first word of the text, written in Koine Greek: apocalypses, meaning "unveiling" or "revelation". The Book of Revelation is the only apocalyptic document in the New Testament canon (although there are short apocalyptic passages in various places in the Gospels and the Epistles).

Now to understand what the book of revelation is, thanks to Wikipedia I want to emphasize in this chapter the importance of a tamed tongue. The Bible speaks that mighty ships are governed by a small helm and we put bits in the mouths of beast to control them, and how many fires a small member kindles. James 3:3 describes the power of a spoken word. From a child we were taught, sticks and stones will break my bones, but words will never hurt me. Is this completely truth?

*Whose word will you hear and believe? First we come to terms with the chapter 3 – Gimel The word "gomel", which begins with and sounds like the letter **Gimel**, means a "benefactor" or someone who gives to others. It symbolizes to receive blessings or cursing's and also represents the Holy Spirit.*

Our battleground for Armageddon is in our mouth, the revelation theory of the Bible starts in our own mind.

"And I will show wonders
in the heavens and in the Earth:
Blood and fire and pillars of smoke.
The Sun shall be turned into darkness,
and the Moon into blood,
before the coming great
and awesome Day of the Lord,
and it shall come to pass
that whoever calls on the Name of the LORD
shall be saved."
(Joel 2:30-32)

When Elijah took on the gifting of a prophet he realized the importance of the spoken Word of God. He knew he would be held accountable by every spoken word or utterance.

A good example of the power of God's gifting comes as in 2 KINGS 2 as Elisha left Jericho and went up to Bethel. As he was walking along the road, a group of boys from the town began mocking and making fun of him. "Go away, baldy!" they chanted. "Go away, baldy!" Elisha turned around and looked at them, and he cursed them in the name of the LORD. Then two bears came out of the woods and mauled forty-two of them. From there Elisha went to Mount Carmel and finally returned to Samaria.

Jesus himself after being baptized of John was led out into the wilderness and finding himself being tempted by the Devil He spoke It is Written twice, just as Elijah went up to Mount Carmel and cast himself down the enemy wanted to remind Jesus, but He responded with His Word and the power of His authority .

39

Because Elijah heard the words of Jezebel he feared for his life, because he gave faith to her words rather than the Word of God.

Our battleground for Armageddon is in our mouth, the revelation theory of the Bible starts in our own mind. I truly believe the last day prophets are looking for a place, but it's in the spirit. But, heaven and earth will pass away but the Word of God will stand forever.

The relationship of God's Word begins as we receive it! No one ever stays stagnant or unproductive in a relationship with God. His Word is his seed, and the insemination begins as we eat it.

Ezekiel 3:1 Then he said to me, "Son of man, eat this scroll I am giving you and fill your stomach with it." So I ate it, and it tasted as sweet as honey in my mouth.

When the root of Jessie was put in the Ark of the Covenant which in Hebrew is another depiction of Word, it was cut off from everything else but still bore fruit or budded.

We can be cut off from everything else but as long as we are in a relationship with God, we will bear fruit.

Look at Jesus in the tomb, He lay on the stone in the sepulcher, also called Easter sepulcher between two cherubim's. When Mary came to find the garment neatly folded and the tomb was empty, Jesus made his way from the Ark to the tabernacle of an earthly dwelling, or to inhabit his creation. He took on the curse of the flesh, and we put on the righteousness of Christ through the blood atonement.

He was the Word made flesh, John 14. The begotten part never existed before Bethlehem, but always existed as the council and wisdom of God, or the Word. Another name for Ark in the Hebrew is Word.

Noah was instructed by God to build an Ark, the patterns and pitches were given. It was the Word that Noah received first in the spiritual that lifted him above the flood.

Noah's battle was already won through the instructions, but was in his obedience to it that caused the manifestation of it.

King David was led to the cave of Adullam, in Hebrew it means "a hiding place. Arabic word adula to mean "turn aside" and Adullam to mean "retreat, refuge".

Sound familiar, a forest or place of wilderness, a place where David received instructions from God. Sometimes God wants us to be led to a place where He can access us, a place where He can commune with us.

If we believe the voices or opinions of others rather than the Word of God, we can become destroyed. How many voices are you hearing?

Listening to God becomes easier as we fine tune our thinking, putting on the mind of Christ, becoming transformed by the renewing of our minds.

Have you ever been in a relationship where someone else does all the talking? That's the way God feels when we don't hear in our relationship with Him. How can we grow when we won't hear what God is saying. When our physical man is at rest then God can speak.

Enoch loved the knowledge of God so much, he desired to just set in God's presence and take notes of revelation. People who seek God will find him and knowledge will be given to those who desire it. Proverbs 25:2 it is the glory of God to conceal a matter, but the glory of kings to search it out.

My point here is, the knowledge or knowing of God will bring a new way of speaking and hearing God.

Jesus spoke to his disciples that we should have whatsoever we ask and believe without wavering. We reap what we speak, or rather eat the seed we speak.

It is not that we are not faithful, but are we faithful to what we are called to do for God. When you understand the weight of your words, you will have a new respect and honor when speaking. Let things be done in order and with diligence. Never speak contrary to the Word of God, He declares what is good for you even if it means going through trying times. It is the trials that define who we are, or who we are to become.

Revelatory dream example with a banner

As we become more aware in revelatory dreams we begin to see pictures, maps, and banners.

On the Date: 07/22/2012
Title: It's in your hand today
Type: Revelatory
Dream Text: I saw this banner in a dream "It is in your hand today the safe remnant of God's promises."

Notes: Revelations talks about the remnant of God's chosen being scattered but not utterly destroyed. How did they become scattered you ask? Because of murmuring and complaining.

As I began to study the Lord revealed to me that the all promises are available to me, but only the promises that are not destroyed by my own mouth. The promises that are left over are mine. I have to learn not to curse any of God's promises in my life, to only speak His word. We have whatever we say according to the word of God. We destroy God's promises by cursing what He has blessed.

The power of life is in the tongue of man, unto blessing or curses. Salt and fresh water cannot coexist, what fellowship hath light and darkness. Death and life are in the power of the tongue, Proverbs 18:24.

You get my message now don't you? God is only limited in His power by you. Matthew 16:13-17 Jesus asked Peter, "Who do you say I am?" Simon Peter answered, "You are the Messiah, the Son of the living God. "Jesus replied, "Blessed are you, Simon son of Jonah, for this was not revealed to you by flesh and blood, but by my Father in heaven.

And I tell you that you are Peter, and on this rock I will build my church, and the gates of Hades will not overcome it.

I will give you the keys of the kingdom of heaven; whatever you bind on earth will be bound in heaven, and whatever you loose on earth will be loosed in heaven." Then he ordered his disciples not to tell anyone that he was the Messiah.

The keys of life and death are in the tongue. That is why God chose the tongue to reveal His working power in his prized creation. Why did he not choose some other member of His bride? Because this is the member we use to curse or bless with.

We are saved by faith by confessing that Christ is come in the flesh, and that He died for our sins. By the confession or our faith unto salvation. Why not confess His word over our own words. His words are greater!

When we enter into covenant through the Blood of Christ we are no longer bondmen, but free Sons and Daughters. We are grafted in as if we were always full blooded family. The DNA of Jesus begins its work to create the image and the genetic code that transforms us. Then we can honestly say I and my father are one.

When we take communion we are confessing that we are partaking of His blood, and His body. This is a shadow of bringing Christ internally. Reading and meditating on His Word is eating and drinking the body of Christ.

We are becoming inseminated with His seed. When this seed has brought forth fruit you began to manifest the characteristics and the DNA of Jesus Christ. You will began to look like His, act like His, and love like His. Thereby, all will know whose you are, because you will resemble your father.

His will and desire for us, it to be inaugurated by the blood, to become a Son, reconciled unto the father.
It has always been about the blood, this year is 5781 2020. I believe this number means, 5 HEH, Behold, It is finished, 7 Zayin, cutting away of the flesh 8 Chet which represents tightly fitted and intertwined with the DNA of Jesus, and you are now circumcised of the heart through my son and been reconciled unto the father.

Entering in to the full covenant of the blood, the spiritual immersion of light and spirit.

Chapter 4 – Dalet The Door

This chapter 4 is "The door" as Christ in the door. In Revelations 4 he declares himself to be the door.

REVELATION 4KING JAMES VERSION (KJV)

After this I looked, and, behold, a door was opened in heaven: and the first voice which I heard was as it were of a trumpet talking with me; which said, come up hither, and I will shew thee things which must be hereafter. And immediately I was in the spirit: and, behold, a throne was set in heaven, and one sat on the throne.

and He that sat was to look upon like a jasper and a sardine stone: and there was a rainbow round about the throne, in sight like unto an emerald and round about the throne were four and twenty seats: and upon the seats I saw four and twenty elders sitting, clothed in white raiment; and they had on their heads crowns of gold.

And out of the throne proceeded lightning and thundering and voices: and there were seven lamps of fire burning before the throne, which are the seven spirits of God.

And before the throne there was a sea of glass like unto crystal: and in the midst of the throne, and round about the throne, were four beasts full of eyes before and behind.

And the first beast was like a lion, and the second beast like a calf, and the third beast had a face as a man, and the fourth beast was like a flying eagle.

And the four beasts had each of them six wings about him; and they were full of eyes within: and they rest not day and night, saying, Holy, Holy, Holy, Lord God Almighty, which was, and is, and is to come.

And when those beasts give glory and honour and thanks to him that sat on the throne, who liveth for ever and ever, the four and twenty elders fall down before him that sat on the throne, and worship him that liveth for ever and ever, and cast their crowns before the throne, saying, thou art worthy, o lord, to receive glory and honour and power: for thou hast created all things, and for thy pleasure they are and were created.

Dreams that create vision:

In a dream installment or vision in 2013, my Pastor and his wife walked up to me as I was sitting inside an old stone temple wall overlooking a great countryside. She spoke my name "Jeff, when are you going to write your canticles'?" Canticles' are exhortations or testimonies of my personal experience or hymns or chants typically with biblical text. Another name for Song of Songs would be a canticle.

Twelve Sons of Jacob – Lessons to learn from the Apocrypha

As the twelve sons of Jacob wrote each one to their children upon their deaths described in the Holy Apocrypha outlined certain sins to abstain from and exhorted them to love God and obey his commandments. I also wanted to have a chapter in my book to leave as an inheritance to my children. In doing so, it is my intention to leave my heart in printed form, so that they will learn to love God and find their own special relationship with him.

In the book Gad the 9th son of Jacob spoke to his children "Take heed my children of hatred; for it works iniquity against the Lord Himself: For hatred will not hear the words of His commandments concerning the loving of ones' neighbor, and it sins against God."

And if a brother stumble, immediately it wishes to proclaim it to all men, and is urgent that he should be judged for it, and be punished and slain. If the hater is a slave, he conspires against his master, and with all affliction it devises and plots how he might be killed. For hatred works with envy, and it ever sickens with envy against them that prosper in well doing, whenever it sees or hears of them, it is perpetually peevish.

Just as love would even restore to life the dead, and would call back them that are condemned to die, so hatred would slay the living, and those that have offended in a small matter it would not suffer to live.

For the spirit of hate works together with Satan through hastiness of spirit in all things unto the death of mankind; but the spirit of love works together with the law of God in long suffering unto the salvation of men. Hatred is evil, because it continually abides with lying, speaking against the truth; and it makes small thing to be great, and gives heed to darkness as to light, and calls the sweet bitter, and teaches slander, and war, and violence, and every excess of evil; and it fills the heart with devilish poison. I tell you this my children, from experience, that you may flee hatred, and cleave to the love of the Lord.

I have witnessed first-hand the evil by wrongful accusation against my good works. Once in my own experiences I had a job where there was a manager who brought false accusations against me.

I initially took them in well doing, however as they began to grow contemptuously I started making recordings of our meetings. I was slow to anger, and slow to speak, which made his attacks more brutish and sadistic. It seemed the more calm I was the more it angered him. It eventually led to my termination because I would not quit my duties, or let him push me to anger so that he might have reason to carry out his plans. He once told me that I needed to put Jesus on the back burner while I was at work because it might offend someone.

In all things never give someone ammunition against you so that they might accuse you.

Jesus was in like manner falsely accused by the high priest so that they might find fault in him before men. It is important to always respond, rather than to react.

When you respond to a question or accusation it means to give thought about what you are saying back to the individual. When you react you're lashing out in the emotion of anger or fear, with words that might ultimately bring reproach upon you.

Remember to always show honor to all people no matter who they are or what position they hold. Remember when Jacob met his brother Esau who was only years before swore to kill him, but when Jacob honored his brother, Esau honored him back. When Esau showed honor to Jacob, the better part of Jacob came forth, Israel.

Revelatory Prayer: During Pandemic of 2020-2021

As I began to read the Hebrew Bible, the Lord Himself began to pour out understanding about the creation and manifestation of His Word.

Jesus (is the Mercy Seat and manifestation of the Word. The hebrew word for word is <u>Dabar</u> (meaning a thing). Ark and Word are the same in the hebrew. Hence Ark of the Covenant, Word of the Covenant are the same.
God spoke and it became the Word or (I AM) and the manifestation of Himself toward us.

GOD was the silent, the ALEPH, or breath RUACH HA-KODESH, (Means Holy One) HE spoke, (the creator) HE SPOKE DABAR (Mind is the Council of GOD) or INSTRUCTION to create. Once it was created outward there needed to be a covering, a dwelling place.

His first command was DIVISION (Light from Dark), we are still becoming separated from Darkness by his Word).

When Mary found favor in the sight of God, He sent an angel with the Word, When Mary believed it, she was justified by her faith and consummated and imputed because of her faith, and brought forth fruit of her womb.

The Mercy Seat

The tomb of Jesus was a picture of the Mercy Seat – Two Judgement Seraphim on each side looking down at the atonement or Blood of Christ.

When Noah found Grace, He received the Word of God by faith, acted and received instructions for the ARK=WORD in HEBREW and a manifestation occurred. You cannot believe God without a manifestation occurring.

The disciples where commissioned to go and spread the seed, the Word of God. And where it was received to dwell there and where it was not to shake the dust from the feet. Everywhere the Word is received with gladness of heart Jesus is there and the light will remain.

Chapter 5 HEH – Numbers & Symbols

11 Transition/Revelation (Prophet)
12 Government, entrepreneurial, (Apostle)
14 Double anointing (double 7)
15 Reprieve/ mercy / pardon
16 Established beginnings
17 Election / Elect
18 Established blessing, Established judgment
24 Elders around the throne, completed rule
25 Begin ministry training
30 Begin ministry
35 Highway of holiness (Isaiah 35) BJ
37 First born/ prime # (3x 37=111-my beloved son)
40 Generation & completed rule
49 Year of release
50 Freedom, Year of Jubilee
100 Fullness (100%) (indicates level of maturity) or election, children of promise
111 My beloved son
120 End of flesh
153 Kingdom multiplication
500 Fullness of grace (5x100)
555 Triple grace
666 Full lawlessness
888 Resurrection
1000 Multiplication factor (multiplying the value of other #'s)
1500 light, power, authority (same equivalent)

Dream Dictionary – Short Version

Dream dictionaries are good for references but isn't there a God in heaven who interprets dreams?

Symbols vary from person to person, regions to regions, so these are a generic resource to help give examples how to research a dreamers dream.

Animals

Animal Metaphor

Alligators
slander/ gossips--large mouths, long tails(tales), bossy spirit (the larger they open their mouth. The more open they come against you)

Ants irritation, unwanted guests, Ants can also mean provision or an example of wisdom according to the Bible.

Armadillo nuisance, harasser, destroyer

Bats dark spirits, or reference to being "batty"

Bear devouring presence hungry for what you have vs.: fear of the Lord

Bear, Polar
Devouring presence in cold spiritual environment, 2 polar bears: bipolar, a polarizing influence

Bees
Stinging words, potential for attack in the spiritual environment, an influence that draws out the honey/anointing, a 'pollinating'

Birds - messengers angels, songbirds, leaders, demonic - research the nature of the bird, consider it's color and behavior

Black panther high level witchcraft

Bulls stubborn, "bullheaded", "angry as a bull" word play on bull as in not

Butterflies translation, transformation, Holy Spirit, of the Spirit, anointing

Cats independent thinking/ willful/ curious /witchcraft, word play: catty Cats, siamese simese twins=conjoined..could be something evil trying to attatch

Chicken bland spiritual food, word play "chicken" as in afraid
Cobra spirit of control and manipulation, higher level witchcraft or demonic

Cockroaches pests! can be demonic, attracted to food left out

Cougars predators, fast!

Cow produce milk, sacred cows

Crab hard shell, i.e. not easy to approach

Crocodile big mouth, can drag you down, vicious verbal attack,

Crows/Blackbirds demonic, listening, harassers

Deer "dear" gentle nature, those who are vulnerable

Dog - friend, watch dog(protector) --if following you, being "hounded" or dogs of the earth--those others disdain, a pet issue

Donkey stubborn, vs: can carry a lot

Dragon Satan, a fiery issue you must slay!

Duck a "quack" a charlatan, unclean animal

Eagle prophetic, Jesus, reference to America

Elephant - large prophetic influence (large ears, big nose) religious spirit, memories,(an elephant never forgets) a big issue no one is addressing (the elephant in the living room)

Fawn word play: someone fawning all over you

Fish souls, referencing evangelism small fish "little" , men big fish (big

Flies - occult- lies, swarm on garbage/ wounds /dead, Beelzebub means "lord of the flies"

Flocks spiritual group- birds of a feather flock together!

Frogs - can be demonic, sign of judgement for not releasing others into God's purposes or their destiny

Giraffe long reach, feed on things that are high-- reach for the sky!

Goats - eating anything/ lack of discernment/ stubbornness/ unsaved, wild

Christian, reference to Jesus

Hamster running in circles going nowhere!

Hippopotamus big mouth, bossy spirit, large dangerous and mean influence

Hornet demonic, proverbial "hornets nest" (a dangerous issue to touch!)

Horse power, movement of God, conquest

Body Parts

Body Parts Metaphor

Arm- strength, faith, spiritual reach, reference to strong arming someone

Back strength, ability to carry/ stand

Beard sign of maturity

Belt truth, or referencing discipline

Blood bloodline issues, death, evidence of wounding or blood of Christ

Bones structural issues in your life

Boils - irritations- things that have gotten under the your skin- a reference to anger

Breast - women: ability to nurse young, men: courage, keeping abreast of things

Breath symbol of active life, capacity to take in the spirit

_Butt a reference to things 'behind' you, butting in, cover your butt!
Big Butt laziness or apathy_

Cheeks emotions, word play: cheeky

Earrings anointing to hear God, symbol of bondservant or reference to

Relational associations

Eyes vision, revelation, the window to the soul, reveals the light or darkness of the spirit

Eyebrows protect the eyes, show emotions

Face reveals the heart, word play: on facing things
Face, darkened demonic
Face, lightened angelic

Feet peace, referencing spiritual walk
Feet, barefoot exposure of your walk, walking in freedom

Finger, index Prophet (finger which points and establishes a focus)
Finger, middle Evangelist (longest finger/ farthest reach)
Finger, pinkie Teacher (finger which most easily gets into your ear!)
Finger, ring Pastor (ring finger, faithful one)
Finger, thumb
Apostle (finger that reaches all other fingers), authority "under my thumb"

Fingernails - reveals the health of your ability to relate, can be adorned or used as weapons

Fingers ability to relate, direction, intertwine

Flesh the sinful element of human nature

Forehead referencing your mindset, things on your mind

Hair symbol of the glory of man-- references your wisdom

Hair, Dread Locks rebellion, could be alternative ministry

Building Metaphor

Amphitheater place where things are magnified

Armory storehouse for weapons- place of equipping for spiritual warfare

Atrium place with a large capacity for spiritual things

Auditorium place of prominence, influence

Bank - a place where resources are deposited, withdrawn and exchanged. a place to deposit resources for the future

Bridge - transition, connections from one place or community to another, an overreaching construct, a safe haven over troubled waters

Building workplace, organization, church

Castle fortress, fortified, stronghold (good or bad)

Chicken coop word play- cooped up

Church – A place of the presence of God

Dormitories place of learning, word play- dormant

Engendi place where David fled to hide;

Factory focus on production to the masses (positive or negative)

Farmhouse ministry feeding others

Field the world, place of sowing and reaping, the field as in arena in which you work

Garage storage, adjunct ministry, place where work on cars (what you operate in)

Gas Station place where you refuel spiritually (can be a church or spiritual group)

Gymnasium place of discipline or sport

Hi-rise revelatory ministry / high spiritual calling/ spiritual heights

Hospital place of healing, healing ministry

Hotel place of refreshment- can reference a conference

House, yours your life, your church life, your spiritual condition

House, childhood home issues from your childhood, family of origin issues

House, someone else's their spiritual life, spiritual condition of a group

Mall marketplace,

Psychiatric Hospital place of healing of mental attitudes/strongholds of the mind, mental health issues

Movie Theatre reveals the vision of a place, place where shown "the big picture"

Office Bldg reference to work, administration or the 5 fold ministry (spiritual offices)

Salon (clothing) an exclusive offering for those with great spiritual favor (wealth)

Salon (hair- beauty salon) place where spiritually edified

School place of learning, or place where utilizing teaching gift

Service Station ministries that serve others - help repair, restore and refuel

Shack spiritually poor or lacking

Skyscraper revelatory ministry

Stadium place of large impact

Store place where get provision- spiritual food

Tent mobile ministry

Tower Strength against the enemy (Christ our High Tower)

Train Station

word play--ready to step into something powerful, place of training, place to get back

on track!

Clothing

Meaning (relating to spiritual covering, attitudes, calling, ways, purposes, authority, equipping, outward appearances)

Boots - equipping for a specific arena/circumstance -- look at the style and type of boot for more insight: work (duh), fashion - may be appropriate or inappropriate for the environment, snow- to negotiate a cold spiritual environment etc

Bra - support for nurturing others, sexy bra- equipped for intimacy versus inappropriately revealing self to others

Coat - what you need to function in a cold spiritual environment! Can also be a reference to specific equipping/ or authority(mantle)

Cultural clothing - a reference to that culture and what it represents (think redemptive gift, belief system etc - if you are wearing cultural garb--can be that you are embracing aspects of what that culture represents or have a call to that culture

Dress - reveals the nature of your spiritual walk! (legs) Revealing the feminine nature, appropriate attire for specific environments

Earrings - can be representative of an aspect of your ability/gifting to listen and hear -- how you are displaying this/what others are perceiving

Evening gown - equipping for a more cultured spiritual environment-- something that requires finesse or formality

Fur coat - prestigious mantle,

Garments - all outward attitudes, behavior, equipping, preparation, external appearances, or spiritual covering, (evil or righteous)

Hole in clothes worn out, lacking, old, revealing vulnerable areas, versus just being hip!

Jeans equipping to walk out a specific purpose

Jeans- Levi's - equipping/walking out something specific to God's design/ destiny (Levites were consecrated to God)

Linen - symbol of righteousness/ things done in the power of Christ (versus man's labor alone)

Nakedness - nothing hidden, openness, freedom, versus vulnerability, over-exposed, inappropriate

Nightgown - referencing rest, referencing intimacy, if in nightgown during the day, may be having trouble transitioning from rest to work etc, also may reference that you are only now awakening to something.

Pants - what you need to walk out a particular purpose, idiom for person with authority to make the decisions "she wears the pants in the relationship" Can be a reference to masculine nature or what is necessary to work in specific environments

Shawl equipping for prayer or intercession (prayer shawl)

Shoe - peace, equipping to walk in a specific purpose, arena or calling, protection in what you are walking in

Shoe doesn't fit walking in something you are not called to do
Shoe- too big or small needing to grow into something-- walking in something either too big or too small (feeling confined in what you are doing! Lol)
Shoe, wrong color walking in wrong aspect of what God has called you to do

Shorts - can be comfortable attitudes, etc appropriate for a warm spiritual environment or culture versus-- over exposure of your spiritual walk (legs) or word play on coming up short in what is needed to walk out something God has called you to do

Socks peace, comfort

Speedo streamlined attitude to move forward swiftly in spiritual things

Swimwear attitudes appropriate for spending time in the Spirit or soaking in the Son

Colors Meaning

Red _Wisdom, Power, Anointing, Jesus vs anger, war, death_

Amber _Holiness & purity vs: contamination & idolatry_

Aquamarine _combination of blue and green, revelatory growth or Prosperity, prophetic evangelism_

Black _beautiful, elegant, mysterious, diamond in the rough vs: evil, lack, sin, ignorance, darkness, death_

Blue _revelation, communion vs: depression, anxiety (can also be a reference to boys)_

Brown _compassion, pastoral, humility vs: humanism, brown can also mean the opposite of green-death_

Burgundy _community, communion vs word play maroon/ "marooned"_

Gold _purity (as in refined) God's glory, vs: defilement, idolatry, gilded_

Green _growth, prosperity, full of life, lifegiving, vigor, freshness, that which is flourishing, new beginnings, vs: envy, pride, jealousy Magenta emotion, giving_

Orange _perseverance vs: stubbornness_

Pink - _childlike faith vs. childishness/immaturity (can also be a reference to girls_

Purple *kingly authority, royalty, intercession, Christ king of kings,*

Scion Blue *submitted will, fasting vs: weakness, compromise*

Silver *redemption, wisdom (hair) vs: weakness, compromise,*

White *goodness, purity, clean, righteousness vs: false purity, religion*

Yellow *(renewed) mind, hope, gifts, vs: fear, cowardous*

Pastels *softness, subtleness or developing vs pale or washed out Neon colors suggest soul dreams or dark revelation (neon colors reflect black light)*

People

Angel - Messenger-- pay attention to what they tell you and test the spirit "who are you and what do you think of Jesus?"

Baby or your literal baby
Baby, boy can be a reference to a new leadership ministry/gift
Baby, girl can be a reference to new ministry/gift of power

Brother - Christian Brother, someone who is like a brother to you, one of Similar circumstance, literal brother

Children – next generation, developing/immature gift/job/endeavor (look at the age of the child i.e.5 year old child could represent a ministry that is 5 yrs old, literal children

Ex-Husband - represents something to which you used to be deeply committed, could be literal, or name

Famous person - research what they represent, what their name means, word play, on name, or literal person

Father - Father God, spiritual authority/spiritual father, pastor, literal father

Fireman - Angel, Jesus, spiritual authority, evangelist (rescues people from the very fire of hell) generational inheritance, generational wisdom, literal grandparents

Grandchildren spiritual legacy, generations to come, literal grandchildren

Husband - Something you are deeply committed to (ministry, "married to your job") Jesus, literal husband

Mother Holy Spirit, church or something that nurtures you

Names from scripture - Look up the reference and what their gift, ministry or circumstance was

Neighbor - Literal neighbor, neighboring ministry, metaphoric neighbor (who is my neighbor?)
old ways, something you used to be involved with, name, literal

Oriental Someone sent to "orient" you!

Policeman - Angel, authority, concerning the law, legal ground or legalistic influence

Prophet Represents a prophetic word, prophetic ministry, or literal prophet

Sister - literal sister, spiritual sister, friend who is like a sister to you, someone of same circumstance

Attic - things stored for later, insight into generational issues, a reference to your mental health

Basement - foundational issues, things happening below the surface-- hidden, unseen
Basement, cracked wall problems in the "foundation"

Bathroom - place of cleansing, place where you process your issues, place where soak in the spirit

Bedroom - Place of intimacy, place of rest, Privacy or Undefiled

Closet - insight into attitudes (clothing), prayer closet, "coming out of the closet"

Dining room place of communion with others

Elevator - takes you to a higher spiritual place (elevation) & brings you back down to earth

Family room condition of family life, insight into family relationships

Rooms

Foyer entrance into house, 1st impressions

Garage stuff

Halls place of transition

Kitchen place where prepare spiritual food, serve others

Living room - referencing what's going on now in your life, place of gathering & entertaining others

Office - reference to your 'spiritual office' (5 fold ministry) place where you get down to business! Referencing your spiritual work

Porch, back history, past
Porch, front referencing the immediate future, place of future vision and dreams

Roof - spiritual covering

Stairs - up portal, or progress in the spirit

Stairway - steps to move up or down spiritually, steps down can also be bringing you back to place of grounding, taking you to the street etc.
Windows vision, revelation, window of opportunity (for good or bad)

Transportation Metaphor

Airplane - something large taking off in the spirit,(church, ministry) something flying high (organization doing well)

Ambulance - those with the training and gifts to bring immediate care to the spiritual unwell or wounded

Armored car operating in something that is well defended, prepared for spiritual warfare

Bicycle Moving forward in something that requires energy (pos. or neg.)

Bus people going down the same road together (ministry, group,)

Cadillac - operating in something classy, powerful or superior (also slang for a powerful drug!)

Car - personal journey/ job/ ministry etc. something you are operating in. Can reference a small group
Car, parked staying in one place for a while (pos. or neg.) sidelined, going nowhere
Car," Fred Flintstone" car human effort

Chariot - the prophetic anointing, or trust in our own creation (some trust in horses) if in the air, a reference to heavenly anointing

Convertible - open to the heavens- revelation, versus unprotected from the spiritual atmosphere

Covered wagon pioneering

Driving into water impact people versus, colliding with the world, Dump Truck carry a lot of weight, construction versus word play: 'dumping' on people

Parachute - jumping into the spirit realm, a reference to your back up plan, a reference to resources/people available when you need them, golden parachute: benefits you leave with

Fire truck rescue/ save/ redemption

Go –cart - fun, but doesn't really go anywhere- (closed circle where operates) If at carnival- word play: carnal). Can't operate this way in the real world (not legal)

Hang glider - individual spiritual flight- directed by the Spirit, high heights- not powered by man

Helicopter - a person, or small group operating in the spirit- can get into spirit quickly, agile, rescue helicopter-- people with a calling or ministry to help those who have been seriously wounded

House boat - those who are at home in the world (sea of humanity), those who minister or work with people. Can be a reference to superficial spirituality (live on the surface- or a seeker sensitive church/group

Hummer ATV (hearts), combat, intercession, warfare

Jet, private instructions, you and God alone

Limo - Others driving the situation (pos. or negative), moving somewhere in luxury, directing others to take you where you want to go at a cost

Mobile home temporary place, no ownership of the land

Model of car can cost of what you operate in, reference the dynamic of your job, ministry, spiritual journey-- what is the vehicle used for? how many people can it carry?
Look for word plays: Accord= agreement (all in one accord! Lol)

Triumph – Victorious, Victory

Trailblazer (pioneering spirit) Saab (a sob story) Mercedes (means mercy in Spanish) Acclaim (duh) Caravan (others following you) VW

Beetle - (love bug, versus something bugging you)

Ocean liner/ cruise ship - large church that is mission minded movement/missions- versus indulging the flesh i.e. Carnival Cruise (carnal)

Police car
Authority, legalism, legal ground issues (God's law or the law of man) If police - dishonest- authorities operating in lawlessness

Riverboat - flowing with the Spirit of God- something that impacts many. Look at the condition of the river to see the exact nature of what they are flowing in! (If water is muddy-- can mean confusing or mix of world and spirit)

Rocket - something taking off with great power into the spirit-- but if not careful could burn up!

Roller Coaster temporary thrill-- ups and downs that go nowhere (go in a circle!)

Sailboat directed by Holy Spirit

Ship - wordplay: leader "ship" , a business/movement/ or ministry that impacts people (sea of humanity)

Skateboard personal

Space ship outer limits with God, mystic realm

Speed boat - powerful, short excursions/ opportunities impacting people, exciting ministry/opportunity/business etc that impacts people

Speed boat- cigarette boat powerful showy individual/group can be powered by counterfeit spirit

Stagecoach - rough ride, in cramped quarters, but you're going to get there! Pioneering versus old outdated ways

Submarine - covert, undercover, stealth, moving in deep things of the spirit- not seen by many

Taxi - directing others to take you somewhere at a personal cost. hirelings, word play: taxing

Titanic - something very big destined to go down! Indulgent leaderSHIP going down (moving quickly without awareness of impact of things hidden below the surface

Tractor -plow preparing soil-- preparing (hearts)

Trains powerful move of God, word play: training, something that is "on track"

Truck, "semi" carrying something for someone on assignment, part of your full calling, transport of something to the marketplace, not complete: more delivered

Unicycle - entertaining, requires skill and balance, but not practical for moving forward in one's spiritual journey

UPS Deliverance ministry or bringing gifts Van operating in something designed specifically to take others with you

Double number double of what the number means

Chapter 6 - Vav - Number of Man

Literal meaning: nail or hook.

This is Genesis 1:1 in Hebrew:

בראשית ברא אלהים את השמים ואת הארץ:

If you take the word for "son" in Hebrew (רב) and the word for "I make" (תישא) and put them together, you have the first word of the Scriptures: "in the beginning" (תישארב).

Here I believe that the Hebrew first scriptures are declaring, I will make my son, his hand behold, behold the nail "will be nailed to the tree as the living sacrifice for many sons.

This one happens to be in the very name of G-D or YHVH also known as the Tetragrammaton. This name YHVH actually expresses the name for Yeshua or Jesus in hebrew word pictures. The first letter Y is the hebrew word for "yood" or the hebrew word picture for hand. The next letter is H or "hey" which actually means to reveal or behold. Next is the letter V or "vav" which happens to be the hebrew word picture for nail followed by the letter H again or "hey" which means again to reveal or behold.

So if we were to break this down, the name for G-D or YHVH in the hebrew word picture would say, Y (hand) H (behold) V (nail) H (behold) or look at my hands and look where the nails were.

Now look at John 20:25, 27.

25 The other disciples therefore said unto him, we have seen the LORD. But he said unto them, except I shall see in his hands the print of the nails, and put my finger into the print of the nails, and thrust my hand into his side, I will not believe.

 27 Then saith he to Thomas, Reach hither thy finger, and behold my hands;

John 1:1-3 (KJV) In the beginning was the Word, and the Word was with God, and the Word was God. The same was in the beginning with God. All things were made by him; and without him was not anything made that was made.

Ancient Hebrew letters were like the Egyptian hieroglyphics in that they each had their own meaning. So each letter of the first word means: in man (son) sacrifice consumed with an open hand on the cross. Amazing!

Principles to understanding and interpreting dreams

The first sentence of the Bible reads in Hebrew:

בְּרֵאשִׁית בָּרָא אֱלֹהִים אֵת הַשָּׁמַיִם וְאֵת הָאָרֶץ

B'raysheet ba-RA Eh-lo-HEEM ayt ha-sha-MA-yim v'-ayt ha-A-retz

Ayt is made up of the first and last letters of the Hebrew alphabet, aleph/tav. In fact, the Hebrew alphabet is referred to as aleph/tav. Therefore, the literal translation of the first sentence in the Bible can be understood as, "In the beginning, God created the Hebrew alphabet and then He created the heavens and the earth." From this, the sages understood that the the Hebrew alphabet was used as building blocks to create the heavens and the earth.

This idea is also indicated by the seven Hebrew words which make up this opening sentence. The number seven, in Judaism, represents completion. For example, the Sabbath is the seventh day. God created the world in six days and on the seventh day it was completed and therefore, He rested. The world was complete.

Additionally, the sages discuss the significance of beginning the Torah with a beit rather than an aleph, the first letter of the Hebrew alphabet. Aleph, which represents God Himself, has the numerical value of one in Biblical numerology. God instead chose to start the Torah with the letter beit (בְּ), which has the value of two.

"Jewish tradition teaches that God created the world in order to have relationship with his creation, "This is symbolized by the Torah beginning with the letter beit which indicates duality-the meeting of heaven with earth. God wants man to actively seek Him out and pray towards Him."

The letter beit also stands for "dwelling place", "house" and "palace" as in the word bayit (בַּיִת). By starting the Hebrew Bible with this letter, God is symbolically communicating with us that we should make the Bible a place where we dwell, feel at home and become the prince and princess to the King.

"On Simchat Torah, as we complete the yearly reading of the Torah and immediately beginning again, we are reminded that the Bible must always be kept in our hearts and minds.

We know that God created a world where nothing is random. Therefore, it is intriguing to note that the last word in the Torah is יִשְׂרָאֵל (Israel). This makes the last Hebrew letter of the Torah a lamed (ל). Connecting this last letter with the first letter of the Bible beit together, forms the word lev (לב). Lev means heart. Studying the Bible, especially in Hebrew enters the heart and builds love for God and His creations."

How can I begin to experience seeking the Lord through my resting time?
Your stance towards dreams: Accept them as a valid way of divine communication, Ask the Lord to speak to you as you go to bed, write down the details when you wake up – show the Lord that you value what He wants to share with you.

Structure your nights then to awaken naturally without an alarm that shatters your dream recall ability.

Dreams even release creativity for discoveries and inventions and problem solving ideas. The subconscious mind is very powerful. Provided the conscious mind absorbs plenty of data while awake, the subconscious mind can process and make sense of the data while asleep. Some of the greatest scientific discoveries in history are testament to the importance of sleep and dreams in the operation of our minds.

Identify and examine the symbols of your heart – Playing the game Pictionary might help you develop your understanding of the language of your heart. Children draw pictures before they have command of a written language.

Note your current stance in life – emotionally, physically, mentally and spiritually. – Current circumstances and issues you are dealing with will give you clues to the background / back drop of your dream. Dreams often deal with the current concerns of the dreamer's heart. Symbols will come from the dreamer's life – What do these symbols mean to the dreamer? (Proverbs 20:5, Dan 1:17) Tabulate your own dream language vocabulary. As you study the word of the Lord you will find many symbols used for specific things. Jesus often used symbols to communicate Kingdom instruction to people.

Apply your dreams to your own life's circumstance first. 95% of your dreams will be subjective. These are messages concerning your own life. (People in your dreams often represent an area in your life. An animal most likely is an emotion in you. Actions in dreams are usually actions in your life. Numbers usually represent identical numbers in real life.)

Anchor your life to the word of God. This will allow visionary experiences to grow out of the word like a tree. It will enhance and increase your heart's vocabulary of symbols. Know and recognize your foundation. Remember God is a revealing God. He wants to communicate with you even through your dreams. You have a responsibility to grow in your understanding of the dreams He gives you. After all the gift of dream interpretation is available to you.

Do not make life-changing decisions solely based on a dream. The scriptural principle here is "out of the mouth of two or three witnesses something shall be established." Prove the interpretation to your dreams by the word of God. They must be in line with and in harmony with the inspired word of God. (Another reason why you have to know and study the Bible)

Reoccurring dreams often deal with an unresolved heart issue. Instead of procrastinating around the issue or living in denial or even ignoring it, you will do well to confront this heart issue and allow the Holy Spirit to settle the matter once and for all in your life. You may need to make adjustments in your life by obeying what the Lord wants you to do. Get it done. Simple obedience will release the blessing of God on you.

When interpreting your dream start with the first symbol. Ask: What does this mean to the dreamer's heart? i.e. If it is an animal: What emotion does this animal stir in me? (An angry bull, crafty fox, curious cat, peaceful dove, etc.) It is better to face your emotions than to run from them. Continue to the next symbol and so on. A correct interpretation will often cause the dreamer's heart to "jump" with an "aha". It will be as if someone just put a light on in a dark place. You will do well to recognize that "aha" moment. Furthermore, ask the Lord to lead you through the process.

I want to insert some dreams of my own that enlighten through this process of understanding.

In one dream, I actually woke up! That's right, in the dream. I knew I was in a dream and was asking the Lord at this point, what you are going to reveal to me. As I rose up from off of my bed, in the dream, I realized there was something wrapped around my head so that I could not see.

I put my hands up and started to un-wrap this bandage or wrap from my face. On and on it went around and around, I thought what is this? Then the end and I could see. I went to the window, and looked out, and I saw rivers of fire sweeping through the city, knocking down everything in its path. I saw sinkholes swallowing whole trees. But, I was safe inside my home.
What was this all about was I seeing into the future?

Shortly after this vision, I began to read about the volcano in Hawaii that was taking out everything in its path, and the sinkholes swallowing up cars, residents and even single people in homes. What was happening? Were the visions coming to pass?

More correction dreams:

Here is another dream on 04/29/2012 that deals with responsibilities on the priest of the home.

Title: Sin in your camp
Type: Correction
Dream Text: There is sin in your camp Leviticus 23 don't just leave your excrement out for others to stumble over, if the Lord Himself walks through your camp make sure to prepare a place that you can present to the Lord of host.

Every piece must be dealt with, everything must be buried or covered or it will be overturned. We have to see that every sin is brought to the gate of our city and dealt with as it is our job as priest of our homes to deal with sin in our camp.
Once the Sins brought forth it can be dealt with, buried and never to return again.

The Lord showed me through this dream that when there is a problem or sin in your camp, as the priest of your camp you must bring it to the gate and deal with it.
Even if you have a child who is unruly and will not obey the laws of the camp, and when you try to deal with him in privacy and he refuses to listen.
As the priest of your home it is your responsibility to bring him to the congregation or to the threshold of the gates of the city and let the elders come into counsel about how to deal with this issue. You have to bring it to the gate. Because when the Lord comes into your camp, and you have issues or sin that has not been dealt with, it falls back on your head.

Anything that you have not dealt with whether it be a hidden sin, or something else you would not want God to stumble over when the King enters your camp, should be brought to the gate.

In this chapter, we have discussed correction dreams, but we should mention open correction visions, as they are mentioned in the Bible. Peter was on the rooftop at Joppa when he experienced a vision of the sheet being let down by the four corners with all manners of creeping things. This was determined as an open vision and actually was correction.

Here is an example of one I experienced in 1989.

Title: Open Vision
Type: Correction
Vision Text: I saw a blackbird appear outside of a window at a small apartment where I was at the time. I was in a state of depression and needed some type of intervention.

I was looking out of the window and happened to see this black bird, or Raven and discovered it was making eye contact directly with me. It would not look away as I studied the eyes. Then I heard a voice, "You don't know who I AM", I will show you my power!

Now at this point you're probably thinking, this guy is out there! Then as I stand before God Almighty a small whirlwind came in through the window and surrounded me.

It seemed that somehow I knew I had failed, and that where I was going was not heaven. I could hear voices crying, and I saw what appeared to be some type of cathedral off to my left, and there where people standing before an authority. It was like a supreme wisdom temple.

My attention went back outside the window, and as I studied the Raven, the Voice told the bird directly, "Take three hops forward". As I fervently observed, the bird hopped 1, 2, 3, hops forward.

I was petrified at this point not believing what I just saw, when the voice once again came through, "You still don't believe me!" Then the voice told the bird once again, "Take 3 hops backwards".

Now, I've never seen a bird hop backwards and never have again since this day, but as I live and breathe that bird went 1, 2, 3 hops backwards, and never took its eyes off me. At this point, I jumped up, and ran out the back door of that apartment and into my car.
I was so scared, I went to a friend's house and told them, they told me to sleep it off, and no one believed me.

The next Sunday I went to Church and confronted God at the altar and repented of my sins. I told God, please save me and I will serve you for the rest of my life.

About two weeks later, I received the gift of the Holy Ghost while in a regular Wednesday night service at church. The energy I felt when I yielded to God started in my stomach, and begin to swirl around and around almost like when you're about to be sick, but not a sickening feeling. Instead was a hot like electricity. Then it moved up into my chest and arms and out of my mouth. I began to tremble and cry out not even worried about who would hear me.

I moaned and cried out to my Lord and God, then out of my belly flowed rivers of living water. It's been 34 years since this occurred, and I've never been the same since.

My family can attest to this miraculous change from the young man locked up at 16 in solitary confinement.

As it is written, He that believeth on me, as the scripture hath said, out of his belly shall flow rivers of living water. John 7:38

Do I believe God intervened into my life? If He had not, I wouldn't be here today writing this.

I would stake my life on this experience, some things happen to us to move us beyond a hard place to a place where God can communicate with us.

My wilderness may not be your wilderness, but it truly is the place "Where God Speaks"!

Objective Context:

Associations to the Dream Setting: The setting of this vision occurred in a state of extreme depression and suicidal path.

Feeling(s) Experienced in the Dream: In this vision I was feeling terrified about where I was about to spend eternity. I believe what I experienced was what is referred to in scientific terms is NDE, (Near Death Experience).

Many have experienced this phenomenon and can be interpreted as intervention. There have been many who have had and written about an experience of going to Hell, or seeing people who have passed on.

The manifestation of the impartation:

The vision frightened me to the point that I sought out God. I knew I needed to change my life. God gave me another chance to get my life straightened out.

Interpretations and understanding of the vision:

The vision brought revelation and understanding that had to be researched to determine what was shown.

The Raven

The raven is the first bird to be mentioned in the Bible. Noah sent out a dove from the ark to determine whether or not dry land existed for the rescued animals and humans after the flood. He originally sent forth a raven, found in Genesis 8:6-7. So, what is the raven meaning in the Bible?

The reality that the raven didn't come back only gave Noah half of the information he needed; the first bird had found little food to scavenge. However, Noah still didn't know how much land was in sight. The dove's return, carrying a branch, reassured the original ship's captain that life on Earth was slowly returning to normal. However, the dove hadn't found enough flora to survive. Therefore, it returned. This was also depicting the Holy Spirit giving information and communication to the Word of God, or Ark.

In the Bible, ravens brought both good and evil. Ravens have also been associated with God's care and what God told Job and us regarding his commandments.

Provision
Some scholars believe that this story is a parable about God's provision for man. God feeds us with what we need (even if it is something as simple and basic as food), so long as we look in His direction rather than at ourselves. When we feel like we have nothing left to give, it is often because we are looking at ourselves.
When we look at God, however, God feeds us with what we need. Furthermore, the ravens were a sign of hope.

They were sent out during the flood and returned with food, which meant that even after such a devastating event, there was still plenty of food available.

Wisdom and Knowledge
Regarding ravens' meaning in biblical mythology, the story of Noah's Ark is not the only tale in which they appear. The ancient Jews believed that ravens were a symbol of wisdom and knowledge, as well as foresight. Their ability to remember where food was located, even after years or decades had passed, meant that they were seen as omens of good fortune. This means that if you see a raven, it is a sign that you should be wary of the future and try to plan ahead.

Disobedience
The Bible also teaches that we should respect and honor our parents, as well as other senior members of the family. In Proverbs 30:17, the Bible states that "The eye that mocks a father, that scorns an aged mother, will be pecked out by the ravens of the valley, will be eaten by the vultures."
The verse warns of the consequences of disobeying what God has told us regarding his commandments. The raven's carnivorous habits symbolize the punishment meted out to an offending party. God does not tolerate rebellion against authority from stubborn and disobedient children especially that of one's parents.

I was the perfect example of a rebellious child, if God sent the Raven to feed Elijah, and sent instructions by Noah through the bird, then I believe He could have used it to intervene in my life when I needed a messenger.

Resilience and Survival
When it comes to the raven in the Bible, there are many other instances where the raven is used as a symbol of strength, resilience, and survival. In 1 Kings 17:2–6, God sends a pair of ravens to feed Elijah after he has been fasting for 40 days and nights in the wilderness. The prophet's food

supply runs out when God sends strong winds that prevent any rain from falling. The ravens' arrival provides Elijah with enough food to survive until God sends rain again.

With this being said, the raven symbolizes the ability of human beings to survive in the harshest conditions.

Ravens brought intelligence as well as resourcefulness. In this way, it represents all those who are able to find solutions in difficult situations and make use of available resources.

The Spiritual Meaning Of Ravens:

The spiritual meaning of the raven is linked to the processes of initiation and rebirth, and the profound understanding and insight gained as a result. Listening to divine guidance, igniting your higher consciousness, and letting go of distractions are all steps toward achieving this.

The broader spiritual connection with raven revolves around being flexible and adaptive and discovering the wisdom in fights you may face. Depending on the context, seeing a raven could signify that it's time to enter a new phase of life or another chance at life. If you see a raven, it's a reminder that you can outsmart others when you need to.

There is a lot to learn from the Raven. It definitely can follow instructions!

Chapter 7 – Zayin –The Sword

Dreams and Vision Experiences

Life experiences are wonderful when they involve living for God. Time after time as I have awakened in the morning, you know, right before your fully awake and you're still lingering between the two worlds, I find myself asking, did I receive any word from God? Then as my mind goes back I usually discover that there was some memory lurking in my mind of a dream or vision from the night's sleep.

It's at these times they seem more vivid, and I can recall them better. Then I jot them down or speak them into a handy record feature on my smart phone. Usually I spend the first hour of my day with the Lord in prayer, and it's these critical times I can ask for clarity about the night's ordeal. Every waking day is another Gift of God so as I open my eyes in prayer, I thank the Lord for another day.

In this chapter, it is my intent to show that intervention from God can bring blessing, wisdom, and authority for living a holy life. I also want to discuss the transformation of our minds by eating the DNA of Jesus. How do you eat Jesus you may ask? Jesus himself said, you shall have no part with me unless you drink my blood and eat my body.(John 6).

Communion is a symbol of our drinking the Word of God, and eating the Word of God. Let me quote Ezekiel chapter three: Moreover he said unto me, Son of man, eat that thou findest; eat this roll, and go speak unto the house of Israel. So I opened my mouth, and he caused me to eat that roll. And he said unto me, Son of man, cause thy belly to eat, and fill thy bowels with this roll that I give thee. Then did I eat it; and it was in my mouth as honey for sweetness.

Let us study the Word and discover why there is a need for us to be interactive with God. To expect communication from Him daily. Do you eat daily? Do you drink Daily? If you expect growth you must eat daily. He that hath an ear to hear let him hear the Word of the Lord.

Let me retrace my footsteps a little so you can better understand why I'm writing this book and who this book is designed to speak to.

Coming from a born again believer whom received the Holy Ghost in my mid-twenties, something I had questions about earlier on in my life. I always believed there was a God, I just didn't know if he cared about me.
Then when my road led me back to a church in a place of desperation, I asked the Lord to save me. Things started changing, quit wanting to smoke, noticed I felt cleaner, lighter, and happier.

Then one Sunday night, I was in a pew and an elder of our church came over and laid his hand upon me. I felt the electricity shoot down my legs, my hands and I began to cry out, something I never thought would happen. I got it, I got it, I can't explain it, but I got it.

I received what the apostolic church calls the infilling of the Holy Ghost with the evidence of speaking in tongues and/or the flowing out of you utterances that cannot be understood of men, but is the communication between you and God, and proof that he has control of your spirit.

The Bible speaks that we put bits in the mouths of horses, and the helm moves a mighty ship on course, how much more would God reveal His self in the smallest member of men. The tongue is the smallest of all vessels, but can set a man in hell, or bless the Lord therewith. How real is this you ask? It was so real, that when I went to the parking lot after church, and got into my car, I could not remember how to drive. I just sat there praising God and wondering in awe.

To this day since I was sealed with the promise, received the earnest payment of God, I am a different man. Confidence in myself, love the spirit, and seek His face daily. Now this was just a predestined glimpse into the course set before me, if I chose to continue in God's grace and promises.

24 years I spent in and under a pastor who poured into me teaching, preaching and instruction in righteousness. Then one day, the Lord said, "GO"! "Go where" I said, "Out"! Said the Lord. Many days went by, then I heard it again, "GO"! I said is that you Lord, He said," have you known me this long and you don't know my voice"? I wept, and said, Lord," I'll go".

Not knowing where I was going, I starting visiting The Vine Church of Memphis, TN, were I knew the Pastor and my wife was already attending on Sunday's after our regular church. I remember being so hungry for a word from the Lord, and most every time I went I received some kind of impartation, revelation, or word of knowledge. I remember being in absorbed in the anointing from the top of my head to my toes, covered in the power and presence of God.

I must interject here that the dreams started when my sincere request to God became intent, and I became so hungry for a word, I would read and stand waiting on some type of revelation or answer from the Lord. But it is in rest where God seems to abide. Elijah said, I sought after you in the storms, and the lighting, and the thunder, it was in the still small voice I heard.

The beginning of these gifting's may have come from a special message I received after I was going through a horrible time. I was having financial and personal problems and really didn't think things were ever going to get any better. My Dad had died and my Mom and Pop were across two states.

I never believed in all the mumbo jumbo and psychic readings and all that, and I would never go looking for a word through a psychic, but I'll share the truth here and that's all I can account for.

It was early morning right before dawn; you know when the sun is just beyond the horizon, still so peaceful, not a sound. When I felt a buzzing, almost like a buzzer on a cell phone, without even thinking I said "Hello", when the voice came through not knowing who might answer, I was shocked.

*On the other end was my Father who audibly spoke to me like it was last week, "**Son, this is your Dad**", my immediate thought was (wait, I thought he was dead, or is he?). I remember His voice came booming across who knows where, and the symbol I received was not a picture of my Dad, but of a phone booth, then "**Sorry I have not called, I have been so busy, Just wanted you to know that I am proud of you, and I love you!**", and boom He was gone. Before I could say, Daddy, I love you! I sat straight up in bed, and said Dad, I love you too! Then with tears rolling down my face, I said, that wasn't no dream!*

Now maybe God allowed this, I don't know. Maybe He knew I needed to hear it, or just maybe, my father convinced whoever was in charge to give him 10 seconds, if anyone could convince or persuade people, it was my Dad.

I always wonder how he convinced someone on the other side to let him communicate with me, or was it a God invoked thing. One thing for sure is I am convinced there is an afterlife.

I ask the question, maybe you have to be gifted to hear, and God never gives a gift and then takes it back.

The bottom line is, the communication came through. You ask how this is possible. Of course as Christians we are warned of God not to indulge these types of activities, but when you're sleeping, you don't have much say over the matter.

Moving on to my visit to my Mom in Georgia right before the Thanksgiving holiday, I was praying how and which scripture I could give before our meal. I really felt a sense of pride because I knew I would be asked to share the blessing with our company. The night before I went to bed I had a powerful dream.

I was standing before many people who were standing in a grassy meadow. Some were close and some were far away. I was standing on a hill overlooking them and was about to read out of the Bible. As I opened the word, I remember looking down at the pages and it was a foreign language. They looked like upside down U's crawling across the page.

As I began to concentrate, I was embarrassed because I couldn't read the words like I was ignorant or unlearned. I felt like I was so new and God was showing me that the book goes to the learned not the unlearned, and I had much study before me. How could I stand up before all these people and feel like I would be able to understand His Word.

Then before my eyes the little letters or upside down U's began to march in unity, right across the page like little soldiers.

*I then realized they were ants marching, as they began to march, they started crawling up my arms and I knew I had to let go.
But before I could let go a fountain of water began to gush out of the book coming up before me. I then heard the voice, "drink"! I took the book and put it up to my mouth and began to drink the water.*

Immediately I was slain in the spirit falling backward into the green grass. Here is the entry just like I added it to my dream journal on that day:

Date: 11/26/2011
Title: Hebrew word
Type: Prophetic

Dream Text: In this vision how was standing on the hill before several people about to give the word when I opened the book and all the word was in the Hebrew text and I could not read it then all of a sudden the word began to move like ants on the page and then it began to run off on my arms and then the water began to come out of the book and then I heard a voice say "drink it" and then I was slain in the spirit in front of all the people that were watching me

Notes: I remember I went in and got my wife Teresa to come out on the patio where I was and told her about the vision

<u>*Objective Context:*</u>

When evaluating a dream it is always good to consider our relationships and feelings observed in the dream. What stood out to me, how did I feel during the dream, was God trying to show me something important?

<u>*Associations to the Dream Setting*</u>*: The setting of this dream occurred in a green pasture where there were people far off in the front of me, and then people down below me where I was starting to preach.*

<u>*Feeling(s) Experienced in the Dream*</u>*: In this vision I was feeling excited about the opportunity to give a word of God to the people that were before me.*

<u>*The manifestation of the impartation:*</u>

The next morning I woke up and forgot all this from the night's ordeal. I grabbed my coffee and my Bible and made my way to the back patio to pray my morning prayers. I sat down outside and opened up my Bible. As I began to look at the pages immediately I saw like a whirlwind come out of the pages rushing back over me like when I was first filled with the Holy Ghost. I spoke in tongues and wept.

I ran in and grabbed my wife by the hand and pulled her out on the patio and said, honey, you're not going to believe what just happened with tears streaming down my face. I was just baptized again with the gift of the Holy Ghost.

Interpretations and understanding of the dream:

The vision brought revelation and understanding that had to be researched to determine what was shown.

The Ants

Give not sleep to thine eyes, nor slumber to thine eyelids.
Deliver thyself as a roe from the hand of the hunter, and as a bird from the hand of the fowler. Go to the ant, thou sluggard; consider her ways, and be wise: Which having no guide, overseer, or ruler, Provideth her meat in the summer, and gathereth her food in the harvest. How long wilt thou sleep, O sluggard? when wilt thou arise out of thy sleep? Yet a little sleep, a little slumber, a little folding of the hands to sleep: So shall thy poverty come as one that travelleth, and thy want as an armed man. A naughty person, a wicked man, walketh with a froward mouth.
Proverbs 6:4

A pastor once told me that the ancient Hebrew Jews used to write the letters on their arms, the ants crawling up my arms were kind of like the Word of God being applied to my body.

The water

The water represents cleansing, and the drinking symbolizes to me of being thirsty, to become refreshed.

Drinking:

The dream was a refreshing of the spirit of God in my life and spoke to me about continuing to pursue an understanding of God's Word.

And he said to me, "Son of man, eat what is before you, eat this scroll; then go and speak to the people of Israel." ² So I opened my mouth, and he gave me the scroll to eat.
³ Then he said to me, "Son of man, eat this scroll I am giving you and fill your stomach with it." So I ate it, and it tasted as sweet as honey in my mouth. Ez 3

How can I teach another until I become sufficient with the Word?

Study to show thyself approved unto God, a workman who needeth not to be ashamed, rightly dividing the word of truth. 2 Tim 2:15

When the ancient Jewish priest went in to the Holy of Holies they would wrap the tefillin around his forarms and through his fingers to remember the Word of God.

'Tefillin' is the name given to two black leather boxes (singular: 'tefillah') with straps which are put on by adult Jews for weekday morning prayers, and are worn on the forehead and upper arm. They are also called prayer boxes or phylacteries. The entire prayer box and straps are made from the skin of kosher animals.

The Word of God should be all over me just like the Ants covering my arms, and in my belly like the living waters and the scroll in Ezekiel 3.

The vision brought new revelation, a refreshing to my life and revival of my spirit and a thirst for the Word of God.

During the same night the Lord also gave me a word, "Don't be an enemy of the Wind".

Date: 11/24/2011
Title: Enemy of the wind
Type: Word of Knowledge and Warning

Dream Text: I heard the Lord say don't be in enemy of the wind

Notes: To understand how God uses the wind, we need a knowledge of the two aspects of the wind. First, there is the natural or physical characteristics of the wind. Secondly, there is the Spiritual characteristics of the wind. One Spiritual characteristic of the wind is that it represents God's judgment. These Spiritual winds of judgment are being held back from blowing on the earth until God has sealed the one hundred and forty-four thousand. Matthew speaks of God gathering His people after the wind of judgment blows upon the earth:

"And He shall send His angels with a great sound of a trumpet, and they shall gather together His elect from the four winds, from one end of heaven to the other." Matthew 24:31

A Song

Master of the Wind
My boat of life sails on a troubled sea,
Ever there's a wind in my sails.
But I have a friend who watches over me,

When the breeze turns into a gale.
Chorus:
I know the Master of the wind
I know the Maker of the rain.
He can calm the storm,
Make the sun shine again.
I know the Master of the wind.
Sometimes I soar like an eagle in the sky,
among the peace my soul can be found
An unexpected storm
may drive me from the heights,
Might bring me low,
but never brings me down.
Repeat Chorus:

Feeling(s) Experienced in the Dream:
What Does the Dream Compensate: "Fire, and hail; snow, and vapor; stormy wind fulfilling His Word." Psalm 148:8

Associations to Figures, Symbols in the Dream: Wind- strong opposition/demonic, Holy Spirit. JOHN 3:8

<u>*Interpretation:*</u>

Don't be an enemy to God's judgement.
When God was going to bring judgment upon Egypt to deliver His people, He used the East Wind twice. The first time...

"...Moses stretched forth his rod over the land of Egypt, and the Lord brought an east wind upon the land all that day, and all that night; and when it was morning, the East Wind brought the locusts." Exodus 10:13

Locusts are always a sign of destruction. Nothing lives in the path of the locust. God used the East Wind to bring judgment upon all vegetation Egypt depended on to sustain life. God's judgment is always swift and complete.
The second time God used the East Wind to bring judgment upon Egypt...

"...Moses stretched out his hand over the sea; and the Lord caused the sea to go back by a strong east wind all that night, and made the sea dry land, and the waters were divided." Exodus 14:21

The Vehement East Wind in Nineveh

The prophet Jonah was sent to Nineveh to prophesy that if they did not repent, God was going to totally destroy Nineveh and all that was in it. The King of Nineveh declared a fast and the whole city repented, and God's hand of judgment was stayed. The prophet Jonah became distraught because he felt God had not kept His word. So Jonah went out of the city and was angry with the Lord...

"And it came to pass, when the sun did arise, that God prepared a vehement east wind; and the sun beat upon the

*head of Jonah, that he fainted, and wished in himself to die,
and said, It is better for me to die than to live." Jonah 4:8*

*The wind of judgment blew upon Jonah's rebellion, and he desired to
die. Jonah thought it would be better to be dead, than to face the people
who would consider him a false prophet. The Bible speaks of another
time when man will desire death, but death will not be available to him:*

> *"And there came out of the smoke locusts upon the earth: and
> unto them was given power, as the scorpions of the earth
> have power.
> And to them it was given that they should not kill them, but
> that they should be tormented five months and their torment
> was as the torment of a scorpion, when he striketh a
> man. And in those days shall men seek death, and shall not
> find it; and shall desire to die, and death shall flee from
> them." Revelation 9:3, 5 & 6*

*When God releases the East Wind, His judgment will be released upon
all the earth in the form of locusts, and they will torment man five
months. This torment will be such that man, as Jonah, will want to die,
but death will flee from them.
The East Wind is for those who will not hear God's voice, nor heed His
words while it is yet day. For when the night comes they will be in the
midst of the East Wind with no place of escape.*

Job's East Wind

*When Job's three friends came to him in his time of testing, Eliphaz
related to Job:*

*"Should a wise man utter vain knowledge, and fill his belly
with the east wind?" Job 15:2*

The word translated **vain** *is the Hebrew word RUWACH and
means "breath or spirit". Eliaphas was asking Job if a man should utter
Spiritual knowledge <u>with only physical understanding</u>. Many today are
aware of the judgment of God that is about to be released upon all God's
creation, yet they refuse to prepare their lives for the inevitable. God
desires for them to see with Spiritual understanding, yet they continue to
apply His Word physically to their life instead of making the Spiritual
adjustments needed to be delivered from the East Wind. They are only
filling their bellies with the East Wind of God's judgment when the four
angels release the four winds of heaven.*

The South Wind

*When Job's three friends finished their discourse to Job, the Spirit-filled
young man, Elihu, began to point out the things in Job's life that were
displeasing before God. Elihu informed Job:*

> *"How thy garments are warm, when he quieteth the earth by
> the south wind?" Job 37:17*

*When the South Wind blows, it will bring quietness to God's people.
When man's spirit is quiet before God, God will minister Spiritual truths
unto His people. The South Wind brings a time of refreshing in our lives.
After Job's three religious friends were finished with their criticism of
Job, Elihu, by the Spirit, brought the refreshing South Wind into Job's
life.*

*After the East Wind of God's judgment has blown upon the earth, the
refreshing South Wind will blow upon those who have endured unto the
end and are predestined to become part of the Kingdom of God.*

The Apostle Peter, who was given the keys to the kingdom, spoke of those who will have prepared their lives for the times that are ahead of us:

> "Repent ye therefore, and be converted, that your sins may be blotted out, when the times of refreshing shall come from the presence of the Lord;" Acts 3:19

Peter spoke of the times of refreshing. The times of refreshing from the presence of the Lord will come when the South Wind blows upon the earth. The Psalmist Asaph wrote:

> "He caused an east wind to blow in the heaven: and by His power He brought in the south wind." Psalm 78:26

The Wind in the Tops of the Mulberry Trees

God used the wind many times in His Word to demonstrate His saving grace. There was a time when the Philistine army came against Israel. This was soon after David was anointed King. The Philistines thought they could unseat the newly crowned king and be in control of all Israel. Although David was victorious, the Philistines would try again:

> "Therefore David enquired again of God; and God said unto him, Go not up after them; turn away from them, and come upon them over against the mulberry trees.
> And it shall be, when thou shalt hear a sound of going in the tops of the mulberry trees, that then thou shalt go out to battle: for God is gone forth before thee to smite the host of the Philistines." I Chronicles 14:14-15

God gave David specific instructions. He was to circle around and come up behind the enemy. He was to encamp next to the mulberry trees. There were probably other kinds of trees there. But God did not speak to

99

David to go to just any tree. He gave David direct orders. If the wind of the Lord is going to blow in our lives we need to:

1 Know His voice

2 Listen for His voice

3 Be obedient to His voice.

*David was told, "When thou shalt hear a sound of going in the tops of the <u>mulberry trees</u>...", then he was to attack, not before, nor after. We need to ask, "What was moving in the tops of the mulberry trees?" It was the wind of the Lord. The word **wind** is RUWACH and means "breath or Spirit". It was the Spirit that was moving in the tops of the mulberry trees. It did not blow in any of the other trees, only the mulberry.*

God is wanting us to recognize the move of His Spirit. When David went up, he was successful because he followed the move of the Spirit of God, the wind of the Lord.

<u>Warning dreams:</u>

On November 1, 2011 from dream journal, these have been well documented as I have become more intimate with God. I believe that this first entry from 11/01/2011 was the first real communication I received from the Lord Jesus as I began to seek him in clarity. I was struggling with the lack of worship in our local church, and then came this word. "Levi", then the next night "Ichabod". Below you will be able to see the diagramming and what the initial meaning of these words.

Date: 11/01/2011
Title: Levi
Type: Impartation to minister
Dream Text: The word Levi came to me in a dream

Notes: The name Levi comes from the Levites who were assigned as ministers in the house of the Lord.

Objective Context:
Age Associated with the Dream Setting:
Associations to the Dream Setting: The word Levi is associated with the tribe of Judah the Levitical priesthood.
Feeling(s) Experienced in the Dream: None to recall

What Does the Dream Compensate?

Associations to Figures, Symbols in the Dream: The Levi tribes
Interpretation: The dream declared to pay attention the priesthood of God that we have become Priest and Kings in the kingdom of God.

Warning Dreams:

Date: 11/03/2011
Title: Ichabod
Type: Warning
Dream Text: The word it Ichabod came to me in a dream
Objective Context: Ichabod means "The Glory has departed"
Age of Dream Ego:
Age Associated with the Dream Setting:
Associations to the Dream Setting:
Feeling(s) Experienced in the Dream:
What Does the Dream Compensate:
Associations to Figures, Symbols in the Dream:

Interpretation: It was during this impartation I felt that it was an issue that if the Glory had departed then we needed to find out why and what I should do to get it back. I knew that if I created a place of worship in my church or home that the Lord would visit.

I created an altar in my home on the second floor right over my bed and began a prayer ritual morning and evening.

Word of Knowledge Vision

Date: 07/07/2012
Title: Stolen Purse/Money

Type: *Word of Knowledge*
Dream Text: *"someone has stolen from her, but it wasn't a large amount"*

Wife's Purse Dream
I had a dream one night and I saw my wives purse, and I heard the spirit say, someone has stolen from her, but it wasn't a large amount.

It was around July 7 and I told my wife what I had seen in my dream. She said, no one can steal out of my purse because I keep it in the trunk of my car where no one can get to it. So I said okay, and time went on as usual. Then around July 13 she got a call from a clothing shop in a neighboring city that reported her card had been used to make some purchases.

The purse was a symbol that was used, not to indicate that things were stolen out of the purse, but it was a symbol of my wives money, or where she kept her money. Just like a phone is a national symbol for communication, the Holy Spirit may use something to communicate to you that you understand and is common ground for that communication. After all the Hebrew language is God's language to man using symbols that we could understand and communicate with.

God knows the language you speak, he wants to be with you and help you. The Bible says that He will send His Angel to watch over you and to protect you lest you dash your foot against a stone.
Psalm 91:12

Relationship of God's Word Dream Impartation:

There was another revelation dream to which the word of the Lord came to me like a rushing flood. I saw myself in a cave crawling on the floor, like the threshing floor; there was an ancient book with tons of dust all over it. That's when I opened the book just a hair when all of a sudden, such light, and knowledge came rushing out I couldn't contain it all. I shut the book back, got out of bed and wrote for three hours on the innocence of letting little things become big things.

The impartation received incited that the instructions Noah received lifted Noah's Ark, every word precept upon precept, line upon line, pattern and pitch. Without God's instruction there would have not been a manifestation of the Ark. Another word for Ark in Hebrew is 'teebah' which also denotes 'Word'. The word of God lifted Noah out of the iniquity of that world.

The impartation also denoted that the small drips that we allow to come into our lives will eventually overflow us, and then as we finally wake up and realize we are overwhelmed in the flood of turmoil.

The revelation continued about how God's Word is greater than our word. When we enter into a relationship with God but refuse to hear His word, it becomes like being in a relationship with someone who does all of the talking all of the time, it becomes impossible for us to grow from that relationship.

In order for us to grow we must hear everything God is speaking to us. Everything in God's presence grows. Consider the Rose of Sharon, also called Arron's rod, when laid inside the Ark of the Covenant, even cut off from everything else or estranged it brought forth fruit of itself. It came into covenant with the presence of almighty God.

If you're not hearing you're not growing, but you're remaining the same. Your seed is dormant. Seeds can remain dormant for hundreds of years, how long will you wait?

When you come into relationship with anyone, and you're not taking anything away from the relationship, it gets boring quickly. God's Word is greater than I, if I speak my word nothing will happen, however If I speak His word, I can move mountains, I can cause my enemies to flee, I can raise the dead, heal people, and the sun will stand still.

Without the Word or Ark, which is a shadow of God's Word. When we enter in to His Word we become lifted out of destruction. It is a picture of deliverance from those minuscule things that drip in unnoticed, that's what we need to look for.

The little things that seem so innocent. In a picture of the Ark we can see how the instructions Noah received from the Lord saved him, and his family from the deluge. Without hearing the Word, then doing the Word, there never would have been the manifestation of the Ark. Without the instructions (The ARK) from the Lord (The Word), Noah would have been lost.

Another illustration I might add is there was a window in the top of the Ark where the dove ascended and descended when Noah was testing the waters. This is a spiritual image of the spirit of God visiting the Word. The Bible says the letter killeth, but the Spirit giveth life. (2 Cor. 3:6).

Chapter 8 - CHETH Faith and Fear

Fear blinds our hearts, deafens our ears to the voice of the Holy Spirit. Fear has control when we come into agreement with the enemies plans. Do not let fear blind you from Gods vision for you. Smith Wigglesworth

We must allow the Holy Spirit to move us into the greater measures of faith.
Faith allows us no limits, no boundaries and no lack.

Things faith will open:

Testimony of elders
Translation of Enoch
Heirs of righteousness – Noah
Land of promises – Abraham
Holy laughter – Sarah
Covenant promises – Abraham
Blessings for Jacob – Isaac

Faith must be active, must be assertive and must be focused to destroy the works of darkness.
Through faith Gods light collides with the temporal inferior natural realm, bringing changes that reflect Gods divine plans for your individual lives.
Tangible faith is not the absence of doubt, but the presence of belief in God.
It overcomes obstacles and breaks through barriers of doubt and unbelief; it activates Gods peace, healing, presence and authority.

Gods authority comes not in the volume or intensity of our voices while we pray and preach, heal the sick, or cast out devils, but in the measure of intimate time we spend gazing into his beautiful face.

Strong faith causes, obscure, isolated, desperate people who have suffered years of shame to press through crowds of people, believing that one touch of the hem of the masters garment will transmit healing and restorations.

We must become violent with our pursuit for healing. Hold fast to Gods promises.

Confusion of the disciples:

Walking confused, Jesus enters into their conversation and asked them why your countenance has fallen. They asked him, are you the only one in Jerusalem that does not know about Jesus being crucified.

Luke 27:27
Jesus in His physical form began to take them on a journey from beginning with Moses on how the scripture pointed to him by prophecy. Through the Tanakh (canonical collection of Hebrew scriptures/Old Testament) their eyes were opened and He vanished from their site. On who He was and why He came.

Jesus was the fulfillment of the Judaism and Hebraic covenant.
Judaism without Jesus is incomplete.
Jew meaning born as a descendant of Abraham Isaac and Jacob
If you believed Moses then you would believe me, I have come to fulfil the law, not destroy the law.

Jew is by birth, Christian is by faith.

Jewish is a physical offspring of Abraham, Isaac and Jacob.
On the eighth day, a Jewish son is circumcised, what does he believe at that age?
He is circumcised because of what he is, not by what he believes.

Christian is circumcised by the heart because of what he believes, not by what he is born. When you're born again of the water, and spirit, that's why the first thing you say is "Abba Father" or by speaking in the spiritual tongue upon birth. You cry!

Even a Jew that does not believe in God is Jewish by lineage, not by belief.
A Doctor can be a doctor, but not practice medicine.
A Jew can be Jewish and not practice Judaism.
But a person cannot be a Christian without obedience to God's Word.

Wisdom comes by obedience of God's Word. Knowledge comes from Understanding.

The Fear of the Lord is the beginning of Wisdom, and Knowledge of the holy is understanding.

You can have knowledge of God's word and still not practice it. Wisdom comes from the practicing of God's word.

The law was given for guidepost to keep us from destruction. Those that disobey Gods word are usually taken in their own destruction.

Acts of Faith

Another act of faith is not just believing God can heal, but that He will heal us. Our faith can reach God even while our intellectual self is at rest. When we lay down, we should say "I am healed this night by my faith in Jesus name, I receive it even now"!

Charlotte Airport Incident

A faith act example is listed below:

Talking about Jonah, how he put the Gourd, the worm and the vehement east wind in Jonahs path for a reason. To be in God's will and the obedience to do just that, can mean the difference of winning a soul for the kingdom of God.
Let's look at the possibility that God could be trying to teach that the act of giving and being used in his will can give us more joy than being selfish and self-willed.

Rather than to always look at Jonahs perspective let's get out of the box just for a second and use the fish as an example of us questioning God's will for our own life. Humor me while I make some assumptions about the fish.
 Let's imagine how he wondered why his whole life was different from the other fish, why he was perhaps larger, or could not descend quite as far as the others, because of his inability to exhale his air completely, his eyes may have been larger and he was made a little different than the others for a specific purpose in mind.

We could even pull out the fish who carried a gold coin and was available at just the right time and season of which God had commanded him, or the gourd, the worm and the east wind, or even Jonah himself for God made them all.

Now maybe God put me in a place and a time to perform a task, maybe even centered my entire career for one event. To perform a higher calling, a specific task in mind.

I happened to be boarding an aircraft in Charlotte North Carolina that was bound for Memphis Tennessee. As I arrived in Charlotte, North Carolina while walking toward my gate, I was tired, looking for a quiet flight back to Memphis.

Just maybe a cup of coffee, then a drive home from the airport. Then I heard the most horrible Childs scream I have ever heard, thinking that someone had been hurt or worse, I began to increase my steps walking toward the gate.

I soon realized it was coming from the gate inside the corridor to board the aircraft. As the attendant looked at my boarding pass, I heard the screams; they were coming from inside the aircraft.

I thought, oh no, I can't believe I'm going to have to ride all the way into Memphis listening to this. As I began to board, I was looking for row 8A, and then I saw the women and her child were in my row.

I thought oh no again, now I'm going to have to sit next to them. Then I looked for seat A, and I saw she was in my assigned seat. Great! Now, I have to talk to her. As she was trying with no luck to console her child I said, excuse me Ma'am, you're in my seat.

She said, I'm sorry, I have this whole row, do you mind taking any seat, then I said no ma'am, no problem I see you have your hands full. With all the screaming I could almost read the minds of the passengers, I wish someone would just whip that child and make her shut up.

Then the stewardess came back and said, ma'am, if you don't get your child under restraint we will have to ask you to de-board the aircraft. She began to cry, she said, we have been kicked off our first flight today and have been in the airport all day, and my child has even been sedated, we just want to make it home.

110

Please don't make us get off the plane, she said", that's when I turned my head and began to pray. I said, Lord, please send an angel to bring this child a spirit of peace. That's when I heard the whisper, I have, and I sent you!
I froze, me Lord, how, I mean what can I do? Then, something inside me said, I'll try.

I turned toward the child, waving my hand to make sure she could see behind the tears, and said loudly" HI, WHATS YOUR NAME"?

Her Mom said, her name is Savannah, I said, that's my Grandbaby's name. I bet you like Dora, and Boots, she stopped crying, I said, I bet when you get home you can watch Dora and Boots on television. I bet you're just tired. I moved my hand toward the child and said can I pray for her, and you, and she said yes, and I put my hand out and touched her shoulder and said, Lord, give her rest in JESUS NAME, while I rebuked the spirit of fear in my mind, and then I said and Mama, you just love that child, in JESUS NAME, now rest. As tears began to flow from her mother Savannah's head fell immediately into her mother's arms and fell into a deep sleep.

Almost simultaneously the engines roared to life and the lights were dimmed in the cabin, not a single peep was heard. Not even the passengers were speaking, I thought this was strange so I peeked behind me and saw a dozen smiles. Then I realized all ears must have been on us. The whole flight was quiet. Then as the stewardess began to hand out drinks and pretzels , the women and child were passed up, I was thrown a bag of pretzels in brief passing, and even after landing in Memphis, passengers remained speechless.

I thought I can mix in at baggage claim. No dice, I was spotted and pointed out. Whatever I thought, rather than to live in obedience unto God than man, and also was reminded of the scripture obedience is counted better than sacrifice.

Hopefully they made it home okay, and all was well. I believe so.

There is no fear in love; but perfect love casteth out fear: because fear hath torment. He that feareth is not made perfect in love. 1 John 4:18

I wondered in amazement over this happening for years, a dear Pastor by the name of Rev. Spencer McCool told me that that's just what it was, a happening.

By faith, I heard the faint whisper that saved the day.

Thank you God for speaking to me in those times of frustration and giving us wisdom and courage to perform miracles, signs and wonders!

And these signs will follow those who believe: In My name they will cast out demons; they will speak with new tongues; they will take up serpents; and if they drink anything deadly, it will by no means hurt them; they will lay hands on the sick, and they will recover." Mark 16:17-18 NKJV

The Campfire

My wife and I sometimes take our RV and go up into the Ozarks and camp. One evening while we praying and waiting on the Presidential results in 2020 we were setting around the campfire discussing some things in the Bible and life, I had brought some wood from an old tree that I had to cut down in my yard. I was telling my wife how beautiful the tree once was when it bloomed and how could such a beautiful tree end up in the fire.
As I gazed into the fire, I could hardly believe my eyes. Burning bigger than life was Joel 1:19 O Lord, to thee will I cry: for the fire hath devoured the pastures of the wilderness, and the flame hath burned all the trees of the field.

Chapter 9 – TETH Fruits & Gifts

God also imparts gifts, abilities and instructions through visionary experiences. Solomon encountered the Lord in a dream and received gifts that defined him as a king. (1 Kings 3:5-15) The wise men who came from the east to bring honor to the Savior received a warning from an angel in a dream. (Matt. 2:12)

The Lord established an eternal covenant with Abraham in a dream. (Gen. 15:12-13,18) Pharaoh had a dream that spoke of things to come. Joseph acted on the revelation from that dream to prepare Egypt for the looming drought. (Gen. 41) Peter's vision encouraged him to minister to Cornelius' household, thus opening his heart beyond his Jewish roots. (Acts 10)

Paul changed his ministry direction from Bithynia to Macedonia after a visionary experience. (Acts 16:7-10)

We find an interesting reference to both dreams and visions in Acts 2:17

And it shall come to pass in the last days, says God,
That I will pour out of My Spirit on all flesh;
Your sons and your daughters shall prophesy,
Your young men shall see visions,
Your old men shall dream dreams.

Peter is quoting the prophet Joel. He connects the outpouring of the Holy Spirit to the start of the last days. He continues to identify certain characteristics about this final age. There will be a restoration of the prophetic gift. Remember he was living in an era where there have been no prophetic voices for several generations.

John, the Baptist and Jesus ushered in this new dispensation. Two other characteristics of this age are visions and dreams.

Young men see visions. Old men dream dreams. I do not believe these statements made by Joel and then again by Peter have much to do with age. I believe there is a deeper revelation. The term "young men" speak of the regenerated person; the spirit of the Born-again believer, the new man in Christ, our spirit man! After becoming a new creation in Christ your spirit is open to receive visions from the Lord as a way for the Lord to communicate to you.

The term "old men" here refers to the flesh, the natural you. This part of you is also able to receive communication from the Lord, but it comes in the form of dreams, when your flesh is at rest. This reduces distractions from without and within.

Other Mantles, Impartations & Gifting's

As I began my journey into dreams and visions around 2004, little did I come to realize that I would begin such a serious look into the topic? But in the early hours of 11/07/2011 I had such an experience it changed the entire course of my life.

Knights for Christ:

Date: 11/07/2011
Title: Saint George - Knighted In A Dream

Type: Prophetic
Dream Text: I saw an angel over the left side of my bed and heard a voice saying "this one is likened to Saint George" and an open vision of an angel pointing toward me, then felt like two taps on my shoulder like I was being knighted. One thing I should mention is that the angel seemed to be "being monitored" by an entity afar off who seemed to be calling.

Notes: It occurred to me that the angel had dark hair and dark beard and was wearing a white robe. The voice seemed to be as loud as a thunderstorm, but peaceful.

Objective Context: It did not occur to me then but later the angel appeared to the right side of my altar below the balcony where my prayer roost is.

Age Associated with the Dream Setting:

Associations to the Dream Setting: When I heard the words this one is likened to Saint George it was like it was pointing toward me and looking off in the distance towards somebody else

Feeling(s) Experienced in the Dream:

What Does the Dream Compensate: This dream was the substance on which the Knights for Christ image was founded.

Associations to Figures, Symbols in the Dream:

Interpretation:

I believe that I was being exhorted and lifted up to accommodate trials and tribulations at work to come.

After this occurred I began asking the Lord if I should begin a work using these experiences. As I was in prayer I received 7 words of wisdom that leads to holiness.

7 metaphor – armor of God, 6 prepares – us to live holy, 5 principles – of God, 4 servitude – to become servants, 3 sharpens – iron sharpens iron, 2 tools – for the kingdom, 1 attractive – to the senses.

I looked around for groups that used the metaphor of knighthood and found one already existed who believed in the apostolic doctrine the apostles taught.

Then I contacted Knights for Christ and spoke with Sir Keith Irons who encouraged me to finish the course work. As I began to study I knew that this was something that would grow me as a man of God. Sir Keith came to the Memphis, TN area and knighted me in a ceremony at the Vine Church of Memphis on August 5, 2012. At this time I was promoted to V.P. Discipleship U.S. & Int. 38 States and 6 countries.

If it were not for this dream, I never would have contacted Sir Keith Irons, President of The Knights for Christ U.S. & Int.

November 7, 2011, by the finger pointing angel, that said "This one is likened unto Saint George", who was this I asked? Jumping out of bed I said who is that? And who is Saint George?

I've never heard of him, or if there was even such thing of a Saint George. At this point I just thanked God for Google. As I began to search out, yes, Saint George is a real person, and who happened to be the patron Saint of England and six other countries. He is the saint of the Calvary and was considered a help to those in military. To this day, the St George cross is given for exceptional bravery in the line of duty by Kings and queens alike.

I felt my interpretation for this dream came in many months, which brought me to the Knights for Christ, established me as a vessel of honor, and caused me to know true honor for my family, friends and church folk alike.

Many revelations have come from that, my understanding about, strength, honor, faith, courage, loyalty and respect, and helped me to realize who I truly am as a man.

I learned that servant hood is where we should strive first. I was praying again at my altar of which if you want a true transformation of character and a DNA change, create an altar in your home.
An altar is where you can come into the presence of the most high. I envisioned myself walking into the courts of God with a healthy countenance of praise. Then moving to the table of showbread, on to the brazen alter, where the seven golden candlesticks burn night and day, where the flames of our prayers never go out, and the smoke and incense ascend up before the Holy one of Israel.

Then past the six pillars of humanity, through the veil and before the mercy seat of God. It's there that I can come boldly into His presence, of Him whom which I have to do. Not to ask anything of Him, but to become acquainted with Him, familiarize myself and know my King and Lord.

Prayer in the upper room:

One day while praying, the Holy Ghost interrupted me and said "You're a man of low degree". I was devastated, how could you say that. I quit and got up and walked away from my altar. Then I was prompted to come back and read where it said in James 1:9 Let the the brother of low degree rejoice in that he is exalted: Then I understood that if we exalt ourselves, we shall be brought low, but if God exalts us, we shall be exalted.

Mantles or Impartations:

Sir Isaac Newton Dream impartation:
Back to my mornings, Many times I seem to receive fresh impartation after I become fully awake. Sometimes I discover new names, or places that I've never seen or been to before.
One dream I was surrounded by some unsavory characters and I must admit, I was pretty nervous. I thought I was going to be attacked as many evil looking men began to surround me.

*Then a short gentleman approached me and introduced himself as **Sir Isaac Newton.***

Isaac Newton Dream

Never before had I seen pictures, books or to my memory received information about the man, other than an apple falling on his head under some apple tree hundreds of years ago. But, in this case as he introduced himself, it dawned on me there must have been some connection, then I realized. Sir Isaac Newton was a Knight! Hence the name Sir I thought. I might add this was realized in the dream and not before. This proves that we can process thought, communicate and receive new information in our minds while sleeping.

Cause and effect: In my case analysis I received impartation from a source (Sir Newton), of a factual event, while my intellectual self was asleep, thereby proves that we can communicate real facts in a dream state.

I spoke with him and said "I am also a Knight for Christ", then that's all I can recall. After a few days of research on the subject to my surprise I discovered Isaac Newton was a man of God, searching for truth in a world of uncertainty. I soon would discover that I and Sir Newton shared many similarities.

A lot of people don't know that Newton had a stepfather and a few half siblings. He had a temper, and was cited for being on the rebellious side in his younger days. Also, in his last days he studied and wrote many articles on the visions of Daniel and other prophetical writings.

It could be said of him that he desired to know the creator and quoted"
"Material things seem to have been composed of the hard and solid Particles ... variously associated with the first Creation by the Counsel of an intelligent Agent. For it became him who created them to set them in order: and if he did so, it is un-philosophical to seek for any other Origin of the World, or to pretend that it might arise out of a Chaos by the mere Laws of Nature. "Unquote, Sir Isaac Newton.

"And from true lordship it follows that the true God is living, intelligent, and powerful; from the other perfections, that he is supreme, or supremely perfect. He is eternal and infinite, omnipotent and omniscient; that is, he endures from eternity to eternity; and he is present from infinity to infinity; he rules all things, and he knows all things that happen or can happen.

Sir Isaac Newton was considered to be the smartest man who ever lived, and had the highest IQ ever recorded. He wrote calculus the mathematical language, and his theory of gravity is still considered valid today.

Newton went further and proposed that gravity was a "universal" force, and that the Sun's gravity was what held planets in their orbits. He was then able to show that Keller's laws were a natural consequence of the "inverse squares law" and today all calculations of the orbits of planets and satellites follow in his footsteps.

What was God showing me through this vision? Perhaps I need to surround myself with people that could improve my knowledge? Perhaps maybe I have learned a lot from his pointing finger! I believe sometimes the Lord and his angels and the Holy Ghost.

So perhaps there is something the Lord wants me to prepare or do in line with what was done with the life of SIN, Sir Isaac Newton, did you catch that. We look for simile's in everything we do while interpreting dreams.

We have already established that God in fact speaks tests, communicates, conditions, and warns us through dreams and visions. This intervention means that yes God intervenes in the lives of His people, excites us, gives us new visions of revelation as we progress into the dynamics of spiritual salvation. There is much more to his plans for us declares the Lord, He desires for us to become more, much more.

Sir Isaac Newton though he appreciated its universalist humanitarianism, he was by no means a deist inasmuch as he believed in a personal God, omniscient and omnipotent, but, above all, immanent not only had He created the universe, but He keeps it under constant surveillance and intervenes in a providential way from time to time (e.g., paths of comets).

Neither was Newton a Unitarian; he believed in Jesus Christ as the Messiah, the Son of God-not a mere man, but a sort of viceroy for the Father (his precise concept is somewhat problematic). Newton diligently sought the Creator through His actions, His work (creation) and His Word (the Bible).

I truly believe that Sir Isaac Newton must have something to share with me. God must think so! After all it is a symbol that I should discover. Do I believe that was really Sir Isaac Newton? I can't answer that, but I can use every bit of knowledge of understanding that was acquired through this experience to increase my growth.

Never underestimate what you can take away from a dream. Sometimes it might be too much pizza, but on the other hand, what if it's a warning of impending danger.

Sir Isaac Newton stated that God intervenes in the affairs of men. I had assumed God set things into a natural order, but Newton's theory still rings true. God must intervene every day to make corrections. It's only when we deny God from working in our lives to correct us we are doomed to fail. Sure we may find temporary happiness, maybe some wealth, but not true joy!

God's Word is a pillar, a foundation, but must be applied to our life to bring adjustment and corrections. The word is intervention.

The book of Joel considers dreams to be one of the eschatological manifestations of the outpouring of the Holy Spirit. Dreams and visions are gifts from God.

Some of the things to pray for are, Spirit of Council, Spirit of wisdom, and a heart of purity.

Knowledge is to know the will of God; wisdom is to know how to apply it to your life.

There are three ways the Lord speaks, God speaking to our spirit, our spirit crying out to God, and Gods spirit interceding through our spirit.

Chapter 10 – Yod Hand & Symbols of the Bible

Number Meaning / Hebrew Reference

- **This is one of the most important understandings of dream interpretation. Hebrew values are important because they emulate God's language and DNA.**

1 Alef God/ unity

Achat [f.], echad [m.] Oneness, Unity, Primacy, First, Beginning. Single and not plural, not subject to multiplicity or division. ($1 \times 1 = 1$) One remains one, it does not change. <u>God is One. (Dt. 6:4)</u> There is one body, one Spirit, one hope, one Lord, one faith, one baptism, one God, one Father. (Eph. 4:4-6)

- *First Hebrew letter: **Aleph** Numerical value of one. Pictographic meaning strength, ox, chief, prince, leader, first. Marks singular future tense "I will."*
- *On Day One of creation (lit. One Day – Yom Echad), light is separated from darkness. Instead of indicating division, this demonstrates the set-apartness of God and His Light. This day is called tov or good. It is akin to being called out.*

- *Also on Day One, the first mention of the Holy Spirit occurs in association with movement. "And the Spirit of God was hovering over the face of the waters." (Gen. 1:2b) Hovering in Hebrew is merachefet (present tense, feminine, singular), which is the action of a mother bird brooding, fluttering, or hovering over her nest. In this case, the Spirit of God is performing this action over the primordial waters of creation. (See Ex. 19:4, Dt. 11:32; 32:10-11, Pro. 8, Is. 49:15; 66: 12-13, Mt. 3:16, Jn. 3:5)The dark, watery Yom Echad is like the womb before "Let light be!" is uttered forth.*
- *The first day of creation is called "One Day" rather than the "first day," insinuating the wholeness and perfection of the day and a prophetic future return to Yom Echad (One Day). In other words, the first day of creation is described with the cardinal number "one" in Hebrew; whereas, the remaining days are described with ordinal numbers (2nd, 3rd, 4th, etc.).*
- *Echad (one) and ahavah (love) are linked, because their Hebrew numerical value is the same: 13. (For more on 13 and other words that equal 13*
- *First Feast: Pesach (Passover) Lev. 23*
- *First Spirit of God: Chokhmah (Wisdom) Is. 11:2*
- *First Church of Revelation: Ephesus (Meaning First, Desirable, or Permitted)*
- ***Negative side**: Pride, Haughty Eyes (1st wicked abomination Pr. 6:16-19)*

Echad (one) is the watchword of Israel. The Shema (Dt.6:4): "Hear, O Israel! The LORD is our God, the LORD is one (echad)!" These words are the first declaration taught to Jewish children and the last words on the lips of the dying. Praying the Shema affirms God's authority over heaven and earth.

*He is the Eternal One and the Source of all creation. But even more than that, it is a declaration that His people accept and reverence His lofty position over mankind. **One Day** is a return to the beginning, a return to Eden. (Is. 46:10, Rev. 21: 6; 22:13) **One Day**, there will be a restoration of all things. (Acts 3:21) **One Day**, God will be all in all. (1 Cor. 15:28) **One Day,** every tear will be wiped away. (Rev. 7:17) **One Day,** YHWH will dwell permanently among men. (Rev. 21:3) **One Day** there will be no more death, no more sorrow, no more pain. (Rev. 21:4)*

*It shall be **<u>one day</u>** Which is known to the LORD Neither day nor night. But at evening time it shall happen that it will be light. And **<u>in that day</u>** it shall be—That living waters shall flow from Jerusalem, half of them toward the eastern sea and half of them toward the western sea; in both summer and winter it shall occur. And the LORD shall be King over all the earth. **<u>In that day</u>** it shall be "**<u>The LORD is one</u>**," and **<u>His name one</u>**. (Zech. 14:7-9 NKJV)*

*Shtayim [f.], shnayim [m.] Divide, difference, oppose, judge, discern, witness, conflict, **blessing**, abundance, **building**, couple, dying to self. It is also related to the Hebrew word shanah, meaning change or repeat. Context determines meaning (as with all numbers). Ideally, two should mirror one, as in the "two shall become one (echad) flesh." Thus, making a true "pair" that works together like one's ears, eyes, nostrils, hands, and feet.*

There are two great commandments (love God/love neighbor), two houses of Israel, two sticks, two sisters, two olive branches, two silver trumpets, two leavened loaves on Shavuot, two cherubim guard Ark of the Covenant and the entrance to Eden, two good spies (Joshua and Caleb), and two witnesses mentioned in the Bible. What is opposite is meant to complement for a blessing, not bring division and conflict. There were two pillars that protected and watched over Israel in the wilderness: a pillar of cloud by day and a pillar of fire by night, yet they were one. These watery fire pillars reflect the earthly waters and the heavenly fire waters of day two of creation.

In the sense above, two (ideally) is meant to bring a blessing, barukh/berakhah, which begins with the letter beht. To bless, in simple understanding, is to multiply something or someone. With the number two, multiplication becomes possible.

When two isn't reflecting the positive side of one (unity), it denotes division rather than multiplication (blessing) in the Bible. For example, the second day of creation DIVIDES the upper and lower waters. The second sentence in scripture speaks of chaos, and the second chapter reveals two trees representing life and death. The Apostolic Writings (N.T.) also confirms two's pattern of division or separation. Consider the second books of Corinthians, Thessalonians, Timothy, Peter, and 2

John; they each speak either about the enemy/antichrist or the assembly in ruin/apostasy. Two presents one with a choice, and hopefully that choice will lead to life and blessing, a positive change that repeats through each new cycle or shanah (year).

- *Second Hebrew letter: **Beit** Numerical value of two. Pictographic meaning house, tent, sons/daughters (ben/bat), to build, and division. As a preposition, it means "in" or "with."*
- *1st letter of the Bible is an enlarged Hebrew beit. **This implies that God's intent from the very beginning of creation was to expand/build His House.***
- *The two (male & female) are meant to join together to form one (echad) flesh, bringing unity.*
- *On day two of creation, the heavenly and earthly waters are separated; this creation day is **not** called tov (good). Heaven and earth are meant to reflect (mirror) one another in oneness. Creation becomes good again when the separation of the waters of day two are gathered together in one place on day three. Separation that does not lead to gathering is not good.*
- *Second Feast: Matzah (Unleavened Bread) Lev. 23*
- *Second Spirit of God: Binah (Understanding- a building, discerning Spirit) Is. 11:2*
- *Second Church of Revelation: Smyrna (Meaning Myrrh)*
- ***Negative side**: Lying (forked) tongue, division, separating unto death. (Second wicked abomination Pr. 6:16-19)*

*Mankind has two natures. They mirror the TWO trees in the Garden, the Tree of Life and the Tree of the Knowledge of Good and Evil. Christians might liken these to the Christ-nature and the sin-nature. Jews, however, refer to the two natures of man as the yetzer hara and the yetzer hatov. Literally this is the evil inclination and the good inclination. I prefer the latter designation as it doesn't completely demonize the lower, earthly nature. The Bible declares that the second tree produces **both** good and evil, a mixture. The lower nature, the evil inclination, is simply the flesh (mind, will, emotions, intellect, instincts, appetites, and desires). Man and animals share this earthly nature, thus it is not wicked or evil.*

127

Humans are told to master or rule these impulses, not deny that they exist or that one can live a human life without them. (Gen.4:6-7) Two requires one to discern this difference. It also requires one to look inward at the heart to see which nature sits on the throne, the shamayim (heavenly waters) or the mayim (earthly waters). For example, see the entire Book of Proverbs (Parables), which personifies the two natures in woman folly and woman wisdom. There is wisdom from above and wisdom from below. Actions, deeds, and especially one's words will reveal which one is operating in the heart of man. (James 3)

The separation on day two divides between the earthly and heavenly waters, the second feast (Matzah) separates one from leaven, and the second Spirit of God (Binah) separates materials in order to build. Since this day is not called tov or good, we must be very careful in how and what we separate. Division is only truly good if it leads to building and gathering (multiplication), not tearing down and isolation (reducing/division). "A wise woman builds her house, but the foolish tears it down with her own hands." (Pr. 14:1)

Shelosh [f.], sheloshah [m.] Seeds, trees, fruit. Revelation, resurrection, gathering balance, equilibrium, pattern, counsel, witness, and strength. New life, sprouting, resurrection, fruitfulness, words of life (counsel), unity, the giving of the Torah and the Spirit, and the foundation of the Temple/House are all signified by the number three. Three brings harmony and unity to opposites like one and two. Three creates a solid or a foundation and makes the first geometric shape (triangle). The sequence of three makes a chain of continuity: three patriarchs, three pilgrimage festivals, third day, three primary manifestations of the Godhead, three ply cord, three witnesses, three kings of united Israel, three primary missionary journeys of Shaul (Paul), three woes of judgement. (Book of Revelation) In tradition, Moses ascended and descended Mount Sinai three times.

*Moses was the **third** child in his family, and his name is often an idiom of the Torah (Law), which was given in month **three** or Sivan. (Ex. 19) God gave the Israelites **three** days to prepare themselves to receive the Torah (Ex. 19) The Tree of Life is an idiom for the Torah in Judaism. (Pr. 3:8 – God's instructions/laws are His wisdom – Dt. 4:5-6) The spindles that hold the sacred scroll are called trees of life and each parchment is called a leave; trees were created on day **three** of creation. (Ps. 119:1-9; 119:92-94; 119:174-176, Pr. 3:18, Mt. 19:16-17, John 1;1-5; 5:46, 1 John 2:3-5) Messiah was in the grave for three days and three nights after dying on a tree (a day three creation).*

*Sign of Jonah/resurrection. Seeds were also created on day **three** of creation. The natural function of seeds teaches death, burial, and resurrection to new life. Mashiach is the "Seed of the Woman" that will overcome the seed of the serpent. (Gen. 3:15) The Word of God is likened to a "Seed." (Luke 8:11)*

- *Third Hebrew letter: **Gimel** Numerical value of three. Pictographic meaning to ripen, reward, nourish, mature, recompense, benefit, foot, and camel. Camels were highly prized in the ancient world. They enabled one to make an otherwise dangerous and deadly journey across the desert or wilderness through their pregnant like hump filled with "water" reserves. In this sense, they enabled life to continue.*
- *There are 3 pilgrimage festivals (shalosh regalim), which are literally FOOT festivals. (Matzah, Shavuot, Sukkot)*
- *On day 3 of creation, the waters are gathered together, dry land appears, and the first seeds, plants, and trees spring to life.*
- *Third Feast: Yom HaBikkurim (Early Firstfruits of Barley) Lev. 23*
- *Third Spirit of God: Etzah (Counsel) Is. 11:2 (Root for etzah is etz, a tree.)*
- *Third Church of Revelation: Pergamum (Meaning height or elevation)*
- ***Negative side**: Hands that shed innocent blood, deeds that tear down instead of ones that gather and build, sowing seeds of death and discord. (Pr. 6:16-19) It's important to note that "hands shedding innocent blood" is also figurative. When we speak slander or even the truth in anger, our words can cause major destruction and damage. Words have the power to shed innocent blood and strangle the life out of another person. This is the antitheses to the 3rd Spirit of God, Counsel (Etzah). Hence, wicked counsel is hands that shed innocent blood. The fruit and seeds from our lips (pens & keyboards) should be pure, not poison.*

Waters are gathered and dry land appears on day three. With the dry land, seeds, trees, and fruit spring forth. Thus, the dividing and separating of day two is ideally to promote gathering, stability, and growth. Thus, three is the foundation of the House or Temple.

Just as trees put down roots deep into the soil for strength, nourishment, and stability, so we too, anchor ourselves in three. One way that this manifests is in our Hope. Because Messiah was resurrected on the third day, we have hope for our own future resurrection.

Because He is the early first fruits (3rd feast) unto God, we also have hope to be counted as His first fruits in resurrection. (1 Cor. 15:12-28)

*Arbah [f.], arbahah [m.] Authority, government, rule, dominion, calendar, time, creation, kingdom, fullness, giving of the Torah (Law) and Holy Spirit. The most holy Name of God has **four** Hebrew letters (yohd, heh, vav, heh – YHWH). Judah was the fourth born son and has the scepter of rule. Pictures completeness much like seven. Four matriarchs, four corners of the earth, four horns on altar, four tassles (tzit-tziyot) are to be worn on one's garment/robe, four living creatures, four horsemen, <u>Four rivers of Eden</u>, four winds, four gospels, etc.*

One the negative side there are four beasts (Dan. 7:3). The fourth one is diverse from the others and has ten horns (see info for the number ten below). Then, an eleventh horn emerges that seeks to change times (appointed seasons/feast days) and law (God's Torah). (Dan. 7:25) This is in direct opposition to the calendar/clock/seasons/law that YHWH gave on day four of creation.

- *Fourth Hebrew letter: **Dalet** Numerical value of four. Pictographic meaning door, draw out or in, knock, path, way, portal to heaven, dominion, control, bough, and branch.*
- *Priests wore four garments: a linen tunic, linen breeches, a linen turban, and a long sash. High priests wore an additional four garments (see number eight): the ephod, breastplate, a cloak of blue wool with bells and pomegranates, and a golden plate on their forehead inscribed with, "Holy to YHWH."*
- *The Mishkan (Tabernacle) had four coverings: badger/porpoise skin, ram skin dyed red, goat's hair, and embroidered linen.*
- *The Passover Seder is structured around fours: the **Four Questions, the Four Sons, and Four Cups of Wine**.*

- *Seven loaves fed **four** thousand with seven baskets leftover. (Mt. 15:32-39)*
- *On day four of creation, the sun, moon, and stars are placed in the sky (natural light) to govern the moedim (feast days). They mark time and give signs. Their natural light separates from the darkness for those on the earth.*
- *God's calendar and prophetic clock were established on Day Four of Creation.*
- *The Jerusalem Council gave FOUR basic requirements for Gentiles to enter the assembly; from that point they would learn Torah/Moses. (Acts 15:19-21)*
- *Four fasts will one day become cheerful moedim. (Zech. 8:19)*
- *Fourth Feast: Shavuot (Pentecost) Lev. 23*
- *Fourth Spirit of God: Ruach Adonai (fullness of Holy Spirit) Is. 11:2*
- *Fourth Church of Revelation: Thyatira (Meaning perfume, odor of affliction, sacrifice of labor, or castle Thya)*
- ***Negative side:*** *A heart that devises wicked imaginations, becoming full of false light. (Pr. 6:16-19) Giving authority to the beast and appetites of desire. Four also results in judgment, as in the four horsemen and the four altar judgments. When the Word is tested in an individual, it will produce life (davar) or pestilence (dever).*

*Ezekiel 14:21 (NASB) For thus says the Lord GOD, "How much more when I send My **four severe judgments** against Jerusalem: **sword, famine, wild beasts and plague** to cut off man and beast from it!*

Four is indicative of AUTHORITY. The fourth branch on the Menorah is the center, main shaft. It is the source for the other six branches. Yeshua stands in the midst of the menorah. (Rev. 1:12-13) On the fourth day of creation, YHWH declared His GOVERNMENT of the earth and all who dwell in it by creating the sun, moon, and stars. These celestial bodies faithfully keep and proclaim His calendar, His months, His weeks, and His holy days to the world. Only the Creator of the Universe has the ability to define and regulate a man's clock and calendar. Our life (time) is limited and decreed by the King of all Creation.

133

Every second of our lives is in the palm of His hands whether we recognize His authority or not. **Thus, TIME and AUTHORITY are intrinsically linked with day four.**

The fourth feast day, Shavuot, the Feast of weeks (time), or Pentecost arrives after one counts fifty days and seven times seven weeks of TIME. It is the fullness of all the feast days as it commemorates Adonai giving His people His Torah (Covenant) and His Spirit (Seal). Again, this is about TIME and AUTHORITY, which declares Adonai's GOVERNMENT of the Universe (this is mirrored by the Sabbath day – a weekly feast day that is also about Time and Authority). See more about the fourth feast, Pentecost Moreover, the Sabbath is the "oht" or sign Between YHWH and His people for all generations, as is keeping the Feast of Unleavened Bread. (Ex. 13:9, 31:13, 17) The "oht" were given on day four of creation.

*The **fourth** piece of furniture in the covered place of the Tabernacle/Temple/House is the **Ark of the Covenant,** but if one counts from the courtyard, it is the seventh. The Most Holy Place could only be entered ONCE in a YEAR. One must know the Creator's calendar given on day four in order to live and not die in this sacred space. The mercy seat is a type of Throne, another picture of Authority and Government. **Four** Living Creatures surround the Throne of Elohim, always declaring, "HOLY, HOLY, HOLY is THE LORD GOD, THE ALMIGHTY, WHO WAS AND WHO IS AND WHO IS TO COME." (Is. 6:3, Rev. 4:8)*

Four and seven have many common factors. They depict holy places in both SPACE and TIME. (For more on this see <u>Rivers of Eden</u>.) Fullness and completeness are characteristics of Abba's House. As the door (delet), four shows one the Way into the Throne room of Adonai, the place of Authority/Kingship. Yeshua is the door for the sheep. (John 10:7-9) It is impossible to get this close and personal with YHWH by entering another door or way. Thus, intimacy and authority are linked.

*Five is indicative of being filled, prepared, and empowered to go forth on whatever mission YHWH has given one to do. Five books of Moses completes YHWH's instructions to His people. It's not a coincidence that grace is also associated with the number five. Grace and Torah are not in opposition to one another; rather they work in harmony with one another. The Torah is the **Seed** carried throughout the earth by the spiritual birds and fish. The five books of Torah are the five loaves that feed thousand with plenty left over for those that come later, all Israel – twelve loaves – like the Bread of Presence. Women have just as much inheritance in the Torah and spreading its message as men, which is pictured in Zelophehad's daughters.*

Chamesh [f.], chameeshah [m.] Power, strength, alertness (wake-up!), Torah, grace, ministry, service, gospel, fruitfulness, going forth, fast movement, anointed, prayers, and protection. The holy anointing oil had five ingredients: four spices mixed with olive oil. (Ex. 30:23-25.) The holy incense also had five ingredients: four spices mixed with salt. (Ex. 30:34-35 – though tradition says there were eleven ingredients.) We are empowered by the Word (Torah) and the Spirit. All is given by God's mercy and grace. There are five Books of Torah (Moses/Law), the five-fold ministry (Eph. 4:11), David's Smooth Stones, fruit from trees is fit to eat in the fifth year.

- *Fifth Hebrew letter: **Hey** Numerical value of five. Pictographic meaning breath, air, spirit, femininity, and behold (to make known). As a prefix, it is the definite article "the."*
- *Five loaves fed five thousand, leaving twelve baskets leftover. (Mt. 14:16-21, a story in all four gospels)*

- *On day five of creation, the birds and fish were created. They move fast and carry seed throughout the whole earth in their migrations. Like them, we are anointed and filled with the Spirit to carry God's Seed, the Gospel throughout the earth. These creatures move in unity.*

- *There are **five** divisions to the Psalms.*

- *Zelophehad had FIVE daughters and no sons. The daughters brought a case before Moses asking to receive an inheritance as sons. YHWH tells Moses that the women are right and they get an inheritance. (Num. 27:7)*

- *Fifth Feast: Rosh Hashanah/ Yom Teruah (Feast of Trumpets) Lev. 23*

- *Fifth Spirit of God: Gvurah (Power/Strength) Is. 11:2*

- *Fifth Church of Revelation: Sardis (Meaning Red Ones, prince of joy, escaping ones, or those who come out)*

- ***Negative side:** Feet that run swiftly to evil, walking toward darkness, trampling the holy with one's feet, being ruled by the power of the nephesh/flesh instead of the power of the Holy Spirit. (Pr. 6:16-19)*

Shesh [f.], sheeshah [m.] Connection, image, man, beast, flesh, work, sacrifice, intimacy, knowledge, sacrificial love (da'at – knowledge), number of man and beast, antichrist, idol, Adam, relationship, and judgment. Six often refers to the works of man, but ideally represents sacrificial love and intimate knowledge with the Creator (Da'at). When the latter is forsaken, only idolatry and flesh remain. One is ALWAYS either projecting the image of God or the image of the beast (flesh) to the world, which is represented by the number six or Day Six of Creation.

*Above all, the letter/number vav is about **connection** and **relationship**. The Talmud says that wherever the vav appears, it also serves to "add" something that is not obvious – something that goes beyond the simple meaning of the text. To whom or what are you connected with? Mankind is a relational being meant for connection. With whom or what shall we attach ourselves? That is the question of Day Six, and the answer to the "mark of the beast."*

On the Torah scroll, each column of text begins with the letter vav (the conjunction "and"), which joins each section to the next in a continual untied flow.[1] Thus, the Word of Adonai in man connects him/her with God. Without the Words of Life, one is disconnected or disjointed from God, because one has chosen to join with the words of "another," such as self or other falsehoods (idolatry).

The purposeful alignment to start each Torah column with a vav is based on the construction of the Tabernacle. Like the Mishkan, the Torah is meant to contain the Spirit or Presence of Adonai. And like man, if the Ruach HaKodesh is not present, it is just letters on parchment, lifeless and incapable of projecting His image to the world.

Exodus 27:9-10 (NKJV) You shall also make the court of the tabernacle. For the south side there shall be **hangings** *for the court made of fine woven linen, one hundred cubits long for one side. 10 And its twenty* **pillars** *and their twenty sockets shall be bronze. The hooks of the pillars and their bands shall be silver.*

The Hebrew word for **curtains/hangings** *is the same word for the* **parchment** *of the Torah scroll. Likewise, the Hebrew word for* **pillars** *is the same word for the* **columns** *on the Torah scroll. In the Tabernacle, the curtains were held up by vavim (plural of vav), hooks that hold two things together.[2] Just as the vavim held the court curtains in place and connected them one to another, firm to the pillars, the Torah connects and stabilizes earth (beings) with the heavenly realm.*

"Six is the revealed creation of the physical world... seven or Shabbat reveals the spiritual within the physical." (Alewine)

- *Sixth Hebrew letter:* **Vav** *Numerical value of six. Pictographic meaning of hook, nail, to connect, tent peg, add to, attach. As a conjunction prefix, it means "and." The number six reveals whether we are connected to Adonai or the beast/flesh.*
- *On Day Six of Creation, beasts of the field (land creatures) and mankind (male and female) were created. Mankind is designed to rule over the beasts of the field. Spiritually, he/she must rule over their own beast/flesh empowered by the Torah – His instructions for this purpose.*
- *The world (all of creation) was created in six days. Hence, six is connected to creation and the work by God and of man as His image bearers.*
- *The first word in the Bible is Bereishit (In the beginning), which in Hebrew consists of* **six** *letters, תישארב.*
- *The* **sixth** *word in the Bible (תאו) begins with vav, connecting "heaven* **and** *earth."*
- *In Bava Batra 14a, the Luchot HaBrit (Tablets of Testimony) were cube shaped sapphire stones, and they measured* **6x6x6** *handbreadths.[3]*
- *The Tefillin or phylacteries and the Mezuzah have the letter shin engraved*

*Mezuzah - on the outside, which represents Shaddai (God Almighty). A shin is made of three vavim or **666**. In this case, the number is positive as the tefillin and the mezuzah represent binding the Word of God as a sign on one's hand, forehead, and doorposts. Dt. 6:8-9 You shall bind them **as a sign on your hand** and they shall be as **frontals on your forehead**. 9 You shall write them on the **doorposts** of your house and on your gates.*

- *There are **six** sedarim (orders) in the Mishnah.[4]*
- *Seraphim have **six** wings, with a head in the center, making a fiery menorah. (Is. 6:2)*
- *Four Living Creatures have **six** appendages/wings with a head, also making a menorah. (Ezek. 1:5-8, Rev. 4:8)*
- *Magen David (Star/Shield of David) has **six** points or wings.*
- *Man is to work for **six** days and then rest on the seventh day, Shabbat. (Ex. 16:23-30; 20:8-11*
- *Noah was **600** years old when the flood waters came upon the earth. (Gen. 7:6)*
- *Isaac was **sixty** years old when Rebecca gave birth to Esau and Jacob. (Gen. 25:26)*
- *Leah bore Jacob **six** sons. (Gen. 30:20)*
- *Jacob served Laban fourteen years for his wives, and **six** years for his flock. (Gen. 31:41)*
- *66 of Jacob's descendants went down to Egypt. (Gen. 46:26-27 with Joseph and his sons, totaling 70.)*
- ***600,000** men on foot (and their families) were redeemed from Egypt. (Ex. 12:37)*
- *Pharaoh chose **600** choice chariots to chase after Israel. (Ex. 14:7)*
- *Goliath's spear head weighed **600** shekels of iron. (1 Sam. 17:7)*
- *In the story of Saul and David, each are said to have **600** men with them in multiple places.*
- *The length of the House of Adonai that King Solomon built was **60** cubits. (1 Kings 6:2)*
- *There were **six** steps that led up to King Solomon's ivory throne. (1 Kings 10:19)*

- *The King of Babylon, Nebuchadnezzar, built a golden image with a height of **60** cubits and a width of **6** cubits. (Dan. 3:1)*
- *The number of the beast IS the number of man, **666**. Let him who has understanding calculate the number. (Rev. 13:18 – see also The Mark of the Beast*
- *Seed that falls on GOOD soil yields 100, **60**, or 30 fold. (Mt. 13:23)*
- *Sixth Feast: Yom HaKippurim (Day of Atonements) Lev. 23*
- *Sixth Spirit of God: Da'at (Knowledge; sacrificial love) Is. 11:2*
- *Sixth Church of Revelation: Philadelphia (Meaning: brotherly love)*
- ***Negative side:** A false witness that speaks lies, being a witness for the enemy or for the lusts of the flesh. (Pr. 6:16-19) See the number 24 for a giant that followed this image of the beast (6) that actually had six fingers on each hand and six toes each foot. The sixth abomination of Pr. 6:16-19, marks a change from body parts to a whole person, a false witness.*

*Peter had a vision of a sheet with unclean beasts at the **sixth hour**. (Acts 10:9) The vision was a parable; the beasts represented people (men), not food. Peter saw the sheet three times and three Gentile men (3+3=6) came to see him. (Acts 10:28-29) This story is a great example of how to discern between the Spirit of Adonai and the desires of the flesh, or the number six.*

How do you view Peter's vision? A flesh ruled person (6) can and usually will twist this encounter to condone the appetites of the flesh; that is, eating unclean animals that YHWH calls an abomination. (Lev. 11) This is a false witness. To their credit, most have been taught by misinformed teachers to view Peter's encounter as a license to indulge in the desires of the flesh. In other words, they've been deceived and are not in outright rebellion, but still a false witness.

On the other hand, one that knows and loves God's Word and commandments will not be looking for a loophole to disobey what is written and will immediately discern the context of Acts chapter 10. Peter clearly interprets his own vision in the text; it's better to take his word for it. The unclean animals symbolize men, and have nothing to do with food or eating what God has forbidden. We must have the mind of Messiah, not a mind set on appeasing the wants, desires, and appetites of the flesh, which is the image of a beast. The beauty and depth of Peter's vision has been tainted by the desire to consume swine's flesh for far too long. Peter's vision is about God's love and acceptance of people from all nations, tribes, and tongues. You must decide which interpretation is spiritual and which one is from the appetite of a beast. This decision is made in the sixth hour (noon) when the sunlight is at its peak in the sky. In other words, there should be no ambiguity or darkness to blind one to truth. See also Dr. Robin Gould's book, Peter's Vision: Beacon or Bacon.

*Song of Solomon 3:6-8 (NASB) What is this coming up from the wilderness like columns of smoke, perfumed with myrrh and frankincense, with all scented powders of the merchant? 7 Behold, it is the **traveling couch of Solomon; sixty mighty men around it**, of the mighty men of Israel. 8 All of them are wielders of the sword, expert in war; each man has his sword at his side, guarding against the terrors of the night.*

7 Zayin/Sword/Perfection, completion

ז

*Shvah [f.], sheevah [m.] Rest, cessation from work, wholeness,
completeness, being ripe, order, stability, and holiness. Also, the number
of the Temple, Adonai's House. We rest (7) in the finished work (6) of
the Messiah. There are seven days of creation, seven days for Temple
dedication, seven Spirits of God, seven feasts of God, seven churches or
assemblies in Revelation, seven stars in Yeshua's hand, seven golden
lampstands, seven seals, seven trumpets, seven bowls, seven thunders
that speak, seven eyes of the Lord, seven horns & eyes on the Lamb,
seven abominations (wicked lamp spirits Pr. 6:16-19), the priest of
Midian (Moses' father-in-law) had seven daughters, Joshua had the
people along with seven priests march around Jericho before the Ark for
seven days. On the 7th day, seven priests blowing seven shofarot along
with the people circled the city seven times. On the 7th circuit, the
shofars sounded long and the people shouted and the walls fell.
Sampson had seven locks of hair in which were the source of his
strength (Holy Spirit). Elijah sent his servant to look for the indication of
rain seven times. Elisha had Naaman wash in the Jordan seven times to
be cured of his leprosy. Elisha laid upon a dead boy; he sneezed seven
times and rose. King Joash began to reign at age seven; and he began to
rebuild the Temple of YHWH. King Hezekiah reinstated the observance
of Passover (1st feast) and Unleavened Bread (seven day festival). The
people were so excited they celebrated an additional seven days. Pure,
white light refracts into seven colors (iris, prism, and rainbow).
On day seven of creation, God rested from His work. He set the seventh
day apart as holy, and gave it a name: Shabbat. Seven transcends the
natural and moves into the supernatural. We begin every week (and even
every day as the day begins at sunset) by RESTING. First, we rest in the
finished work of God, then we go to work (perform good deeds). This
has been G-d's pattern from the very beginning. Rest, then work. Any*

other pattern proclaims mankind's desire to rest in the work of his own hands.

"Six is the revealed creation of the physical world... seven or Shabbat reveals the spiritual within the physical. The Sabbath seven exposes the spirit that moves inside the physical garment of the six." (Alewine) According to the ancient near eastern (ANE) culture and understanding of the cosmos (this includes ancient Israel), seven was the normal operation and order of G-d's House/Temple. Thus, all the seven's in the Bible have to do with Temple building, inauguration, and dedication. (Obviously, the negative side of this is wickedness that destroys this imagery.) For example, the seven days of creation are the seven days of Temple dedication, with Shabbat being the inauguration or rest. In this case, the Shabbat signifies the Creator's rule of heaven and earth and His Temple/presence being the ultimate means of stability and order in the world. In other words, the completeness pictured in the number seven is qualified in ANE thought by TEMPLE building/dedication/inauguration. Without the Temple (G-d's rule), there is chaos and a lack of order in the world. Knowing this should broaden our perspective on the spiritual implication of the number seven. (For more information, see Dr. Dinah Dye's book, The Temple Revealed in Creation

- *Seventh Hebrew letter:* **Zayin** *Numerical value of seven. Pictographic meaning plowshare, weapon, sword, to arm, to adorn, to cut, to feed, completion.*
- *The first verse of the Bible has seven Hebrew words with twenty-eight (4×7) letters.*
- *Blood was sprinkled on the mercy seat seven times on Yom Kippur. (Lev. 16:14) Blood of the chatat (sin) offering was sprinkled before the veil seven times (Lev. 9:17)*
- *It takes seven days to atone for the altar and to purify it. (Ex. 29:37, Ezek. 43:26)*
- *Seven of the Ten Commandments are negative and begin with the Hebrew loh, or no/not, as in "Thou shall not."*
- *Seven weeks (7 x 7) are counted to get to Shavuot (Pentecost). Likewise, 7 x 7 years are counted to reach a Yovel (Jubilee) year.*

Each of these seven year bundles are a Shemittah year or a year of release. (See future post on the number fifty.)

- *Wisdom has seven pillars. (Pr. 9:1)*
- *Seven loaves fed four thousand with seven baskets leftover. (Mt. 15:32-39)*
- *We must forgive our brothers/sisters 7 x 7 times. (Mt. 18:21; Luke 17:4)*
- *Mary Magdalene had seven evil spirits cast from her. (Mar. 16:9, Pr. 6:16-19)*
- *Seventh Feast: Sukkot (Tabernacles) Lev. 23*
- *Seventh Spirit of God: Yirat Adonai (Fear/Reverence of God) Is. 11:2*
- *Seventh Church of Revelation: Laodicea (Meaning justice or vengeance of the people)*
- ***Negative side:** One who sows discord or strife among brothers, tearing down the house. The opposite of restoration and rest. Chaos in the house and in relationships. Becoming wholly wicked. (Pr. 6:16-19) Destroying G-d's Temple or House. Destroying creation, order, stability, and life. Rejecting the Kingdom and YHWH/Yeshua as King. Cup of iniquity, abominations, and wickedness becoming full, which results in destruction.*

The harlot in the Book of Revelation rides a scarlet beast (see number 6) that has SEVEN heads. She is the epitome of one ruled by the image of the beast created on day six and the lusts of the flesh (the beast is red like Esau). The beast has ten horns (see 10 below), which denotes a completely wicked assembly. Instead of holding the holy Shabbat (7) Kiddush cup, she has a cup full of abominations. (Pr. 6:16-19)

Shemoni [f.], shemonah [m.] Literally to "make fat." New beginnings, not just complete (like seven), but satiated. Becoming "fat" is having more than enough. Full to overflowing. Moves from natural to supernatural. Transcends natural time and space to supernatural realm. Figuratively, eight takes one through a full cycle of seven, and begins anew – the One Day – Yom Echad – of creation. But, it also alludes to greater authority (doubled 4), accountability, and holiness (set apartness).

*Torah Portion Shemini – "Eighth" (Lev. 9:1-11:47) describes what occurs "on the eighth day" after the inauguration of the Tabernacle. Aaron's sons brought an **esh zarah**, a strange fire, before Adonai and His fire consumed them. There is a connection between the brazen altar and the incense altar (the latter being the offering of Aaron's sons). Both discern between the spirit and the nephesh. While some nephesh might remain after passing through the brazen altar, none can be present at the golden altar, which is closer to the Presence of the Holy One. For YHWH our God is a consuming fire; He is a jealous God. (Dt. 4:24) His priests are required to teach the people the difference between the holy and the profane. (Lev. 10:10-11)*

While "new beginnings" sound wonderful to the soul, it is imperative that one considers the cost for this to occur. All new life, new births, and new beginnings require a death (at least figuratively). The old must die in order for new life or for a new beginning to occur. The nephesh hates this message, because it does not want to relinquish the power of the soul, the power of sin, to God's holy fire/altar. The ego wars against letting go, to submission, and obedience, because it cannot see past the natural, earthy realm.

It doesn't understand that the smoke rising up from its demise IS the Way to the heavenly realm, and true life. The sign of the covenant, circumcision, which is performed on the "eighth" day, teaches this same message. Saul and David are figures of the desires of the nephesh and the spirit, respectively. It's not a coincidence that David was an "Eighth" son.

There is a distinction, a division, a set-apartness involved with "eight." Holiness is, in a sense, a boundary – or rather, a set of boundaries. There are levels of holiness explained in intricate detail in the Torah (Instructions) of God. Even at Mt. Sinai, the children of Israel were told not to cross the boundary set by Adonai, even in their zeal to gaze upon Him, or they would die. (Ex. 19) In our current state, God's holiness would consume us. Until the final redemption, the redemption of our bodies (resurrection/change), we will suffer the same fate as Nadab and Abihu if we try to zealously cross a holiness boundary beyond what Adonai has prescribed for us. (Rom. 8:18-30, Eph. 4:30-32)

The priesthood had to live by stricter standards than average Israelites. Their boundaries were not as "loose," because they were mediators and drew closer to the Holy One.

Aside from this most holy duty, they were to teach the people the difference between the holy and the profane, and the clean and the unclean. These were/are God's standards, not mans carnal man is deeply opposed to such laws and standards, because these things are Holy and Spiritual, and man is not. (Rom. 7:12-24)

The holiness of Adonai and His Torah are spiritually discerned, a carnal man cannot know them. (1 Cor. 2:14) Failing to teach these spiritual instructions to Adonai's people does "violence" to His Torah, and profanes His Name.

Ezekiel 22:26 (NASB) "Her priests have done violence to My law and have profaned My holy things; they have made no distinction between the holy and the profane, and they have not taught the difference between the unclean and the clean; and they hide their eyes from My sabbaths, and I am profaned among them."

It is important to read the entirety of portion Shemini. The last half explains the distinctions between clean and unclean animals. This is not disconnected from what happened on the "eighth day" with Nadab and Abihu. The Christian world has mostly ignored or explained these laws away to conform to the desires of the nephesh (flesh). But, it is in this section that Adonai twice declares, "Be holy, because I am holy." (Lev. 11:45-46) Food, what one "eats," is deeply intimate. We are to make distinctions, based on what the Word of God says, between the creatures we eat, because they become a part of us (physical body). The spiritual counterpart is even more vital. We are to "eat" the Bread of God, the heavenly bread, which is His Word and Messiah, so it/He becomes a part of us too. This is what sustains, preserves, and allows life to continue in us in both the natural and spiritual realms.

Be holy, be set apart, live by the boundaries declared from the mouth of Adonai in regard to food. Then, consider that only some "clean" creatures were fit to be placed on God's holy altar – another, tighter boundary (holiness). These animals represented the offeror. Closely consider their natural aspects. Cows, goats, and sheep have "cloven hoofs" or feet. They are divided or separated in two, a distinction, akin to holiness and discernment. They also chew the cud. Study that process and relate to the Word of God, the word of His ministers, and the things you "consume." What does this teach us, spiritually? The swine or pigs have feet that look "clean," but they do not chew the cud. They are a figure of deception, hypocrisy, rebellion, and "strangeness." Many years of my life, I could say that I resembled this unclean creature, because while I might have had cloven hoofs, I did not "chew the cud." I ate anything – in both the physical and spiritual sense. I did not ruminate, meditate, or cut, divide, and separate what I was consuming (physically and spiritually), which means the desirable and undesirable both mixed together in my being to became one with me. I ate whatever came my way, just as the swine does. God's people are to make a distinction between such things, even spiritual things, like the Bereans. (Acts 17:10-12)

Want a New Beginning? Make distinctions between the holy and profane, the clean and the unclean. Let those things that war against "it is written" in you DIE by the Letter, so the Spirit can quicken you to Life.

- *Eighth Hebrew letter: **Chet** Numerical value of eight. Pictographic meaning wall, fence, protect, new beginning, separation, sin, outside, olam haba.*
- *Covenant (pictured in circumcision on the 8th day).*
- *The Tabernacle was dedicated in an **eight**-day ceremony.*
- *High Priests wore eight garments: a linen tunic, linen breeches, a linen turban, and a long sash, the ephod, breastplate, a cloak of blue wool with bells and pomegranates, and a golden plate on their forehead inscribed with, "Holy to YHWH."*
- *Righteous King Josiah began his rule of Judah at the age of **eight**. (2 Kings 22:1-2) In the **eighth** year of his reign, while still a boy, he sought YHWH and began to purge Judah of high places and Asherim. (2 Chr. 34:3) He repaired the Temple, discovered the Torah, repented, and cleansed Judah further in the **eighteenth** year of his reign. (2 Kings 22:3 – 23:20) Also in his **eighteenth** year, he restored YHWH's **Passover** (1st feast – see one). With Unleavened Bread, Passover week is EIGHT days, which mirrors the eight day festival of Sukkot plus Shemini Atzeret. (2 Kings 23: 21-25)*
- ***Eight** days after His resurrection, Yeshua appeared to the disciples and spoke to (doubting) Thomas. Thomas proclaimed Yeshua "My Lord and my God." (John 20:26-29)*
- *The Transfiguration occurred on the eighth day (Luke 9:28); and Peter wanted to build three sukkot (tabernacles) for Yeshua, Moses, and Elijah. This is a direct reference to the season of the transfiguration: Sukkot – the eight-day feast of YHWH. It also reveals the realm outside of natural time and space – the future One Day – Yom Echad.*
- *Torah (Law) is elevated to the spiritual realm in Ps. 119 by following an 8 verse alphabetical sequence. (See also Ps. 19:7)*

Paul says, "the Law is Spiritual" in Romans 7:14, indicating that it is spiritually discerned to the natural realm of carnal flesh.

- *Elijah performed eight miracles; and Elisha doubled that with sixteen (8 + 8).*
- ***Eight** souls were saved from the flood in Noah's day, a new beginning.*
- *Chanukah (a late Sukkot festival) is eight days long. Its themes are overcoming darkness with LIGHT, heavenly miracles, supernatural oil, cleansing the Temple, defeating the enemy and idol worship, etc.*
- *Shemini Atzeret, the last great **8th** day of Sukkot asks one to linger (add to over flowing) one more day with YHWH.*
- *King David, a prefigure of Messiah Yeshua, was the eighth son of Jesse (a multiple of four [number for scepter, government, authority, and rule]). (1 Sam. 17: 12-14)*

Eight is passes the completed work of seven and moves one into the realm of the supernatural or the world to come. It also depicts new beginnings as Hebraic thought sees time and the calendar as cyclical, rather than linear. It is a doubling of four or authority and government. Thus, eight is a re-creation of the House/Tabernacle/Temple of YHWH. Coupled with the letter "yohd" (also the symbol for 10), creates the Hebrew word chai or LIFE. It is impossible to get to this level of closeness with Adonai without complete submission and obedience, as demonstrated by Yeshua.

9 Tet/Judgment, (Evangelist)

Tehshah [f.], teeshah [m.] Last and largest single digit. Signifies finality, judgment, harvest, fruitfulness, the womb, duality (good/evil), concealment, truth, loving-kindness, fruit of the Spirit, turning to look upon/gaze, hour of prayer, etc. When nine reveals what it conceals inside, there is fruitfulness, multiplication, and the building of the House.

- *Ninth Hebrew letter:* **Tet** *Numerical value of nine. Pictographic meaning basket, good/evil, snake, surround, knot, twist, spiral, fruitfulness, repentance, judgment.*
- *There are nine* **fruit** *and* **gifts** *of the Spirit. (Gal. 5:22-23, 1 Cor. 12:8-10)*
- *Human gestation lasts nine months, linking the number nine to birth, fruit, and life.*
- *Feast cycle covers nine months, again linking nine to birth (salvation), fruit, and life.*
- *Chanukah (Feast of Dedication) falls in the ninth Hebrew month (Kislev).*
- *The chanukiah menorah has nine branches, which represents the normal seven branched menorah that in tradition, miraculously stayed lit for eight days with only enough oil for one day. The ninth branch is the shamash or servant candle that lights the eight days.*
- *Ninth hour is the hour of prayer in Acts 3:1; 10:30.*
- *Yeshua gave up His Spirit at the ninth hour, securing life for the world. (Mt. 27:46)*
- *Cornelius saw an angel of God in a vision at the* **ninth** *hour. (Acts 10:3, 30)*
- *Nine has mathematical properties unlike any other number.*

- *The first recorded biblical **war** involved four kings against five kings, which equals nine (4+5=9).*
- *Abram was **99** when YHWH changed his name to Abraham, gave him the covenant of circumcision, and predicted Isaac's birth. (Gen. 17)*
- *Sarai was **90** when YHWH changed her name to Sarah and was promised a son (Isaac). (Gen. 17)*
- *Yeshua will leave the 99 sheep to go after one. (Mt. 18:12)*
- *Out of ten cleansed lepers, **nine** do not give praise to God. (Luke 17, **one foreigner** does give praise!)*
- *End time harvest is marked by wars and rumors of war and great judgment. A harvest cannot be made without separating the wheat from the chaff or without putting a sickle to the heads of grain. (Hence, nine's association with judgment.)*
- *The last Nine weeks of the Three Weeks, culminating with Tisha B'Av mark an intensified time of mourning for sin and rebellion, which resulted in the destruction of the first and second Temple on the 9th of Av.*

Esehr [f.], ahsahrah [m.] Divine order, completed cycle, measure, or group (congregation) whether for good or evil, blessing or judgment. A tenth part represents the whole in a tithe. Thus, ten represents a complete congregation, body, or kingdom, whether good or evil.
The orig. meaning of this base prob. was 'gathering, collection, union'. cp. Arab. 'ashara (= he formed a community), 'ashirah (= tribe), ma'ashar (=a group of ten men). Accordingly, Heb. רשע (eser), Arab. 'ashr, etc. prob. meant orig. 'a group collection', whence 'a group of ten', and ultimately 'ten'.

- *Tenth Hebrew letter:* **Yohd** *Numerical value of ten. Pictographic meaning hand, work, worship, deeds, fist, power, congregation. Shows the possessive singular and past singular.*
- *Ten Commandments or Ten Words*
- *Ten Plagues*
- *Abraham endured ten trials.*
- *For the sake of ten righteous people, YHWH would have spared Sodom. (Gen. 18)*
- *Abraham's servant brought ten camels as gifts to Rebecca. He knew she was the one because she watered them. (Gen, 24) Her brother (Laban) and her mother wanted her tarry with them for ten days. Could these represent the Ten Words and what helps the Bride to endure the wilderness until she meets her Groom?*
- *Laban changed Jacob's wages ten times. (Gen. 31:7)*
- *Ten of Joseph's brothers had to go down to Egypt to buy grain because of famine. (Gen. 42:3) Joseph sent them back with ten donkeys loaded with goods and ten female donkeys loaded with grain. (Gen, 45:23)*

- *On the tenth of the month of Aviv (Nisan), lambs were set-apart for each household and inspected for the Passover sacrifice. (Ex. 12) This was mirrored by Yeshua's triumphal entry into Jerusalem on the tenth of Aviv as the sacrificial Lamb of G-d. He was also "inspected" in the four days before Passover as the Lamb of God. (Mt. 21:1-11, Mark 11:1-11, Luke 19:28-44, John 12)*

- *Israel rebelled ten times in the wilderness. (Num. 14:22)*

- *Israelites gathered at least ten homers of quail in the wilderness. Those that ate it died with the meat between their teeth. (Num. 11:32)*
- *There were **10** of 12 **spies** that gave a bad report to Israel, costing them forty more years (4 x 10) in the wilderness.*

- *Foundation of Tabernacle was made from 10 x 10 silver sockets.*
- *Fire came down from heaven ten times (six were in judgment).*

- *Boaz sat before **TEN men (elders/rulers)** at the city gate to redeem the field of Naomi (Elimelech) and also to take Ruth as his wife to carry on the name of his deceased relative (Levirate marriage), Mahlon. (Ruth 4)*

- *Ten Virgins (5 wise, 5 foolish).*

- *Ten lost tribes of Israel.*

- *Wicked Haman had TEN sons. (Esther 9:12)*
- *Tenth generation represented whole. (Dt. 23:3)*
- *Ten generations from Adam to Noah.*
- *Minyan is made complete with ten men for prayer.*
- *Ten Days of Awe between Rosh Hashanah and Yom Kippur.*
- *Day of Atonement falls on tenth day of Tishrei.*

- In the Parable of the Lost Coin (Luke 15:8-10), the woman has a total of TEN silver coins. (Silver is the metal/color of redemption.) When she loses one, she lights a LAMP and sweeps the HOUSE, until she finds the lost coin. Then, she and the entire community rejoices at finding the "lost" coin.
- The beast that the harlot rides in Revelation has seven heads and TEN horns, as does the fourth beast in Daniel's night visions (Dan.7). The horns represent wicked kings or rulers (authority and power).

*Thus says the LORD of hosts, "In those days **ten men from all the nations will grasp the garment of a Jew**, saying, 'Let us go with you, for we have heard that God is with you.'" (Zec. 8:23 NASB)*

<u>**Examples of People who changed the world with impartation from dreams.**</u>

Dreams – Words of Knowledge and Impartation

Dreams have inspired and even given people access to knowledge that they would not have otherwise conceived due to supernatural resources coming straight from God. For example, I have included a few, but there are way too many to list here, but I picked a few of my favorites.

Edgar Cayce – Sleeping Prophet

Throughout history there have been valid accounts of dreamers who have received supernatural information from dreams and visions. I have listed a few for examples of such people that exhibited these abilities other than what is outlined in Biblical prophecy.

The first is none other than Edgar Cayce (pronounced Kay-Cee, 1877-1945) has been called the "sleeping prophet," the "father of holistic medicine," and the most documented psychic of the 20th century. For more than 40 years of his adult life, Cayce gave psychic "readings" to thousands of seekers while in an unconscious state, diagnosing illnesses and revealing lives lived in the past and prophecies yet to come. But who, exactly, was Edgar Cayce?

Many people are surprised to learn that Edgar Cayce was a devoted churchgoer and Sunday school teacher. At a young age, Cayce vowed to read the Bible for every year of his life, and at the time of his death in 1945, he had accomplished this task. Perhaps the readings said it best, when asked how to become psychic, Cayce's advice was to become more spiritual.

Although Cayce died more than 60 years ago, the timeliness of the material in the readings — with subjects like discovering your mission in life, developing your intuition, exploring ancient mysteries, and taking responsibility for your health — is evidenced by the hundreds of books that have been written on the various aspects of this work as well as the dozen or so titles focusing on Cayce's life itself. Together, these books contain information so valuable that even Edgar Cayce himself might have hesitated to predict their impact on the contemporary world.

In 1945, the year of his passing, who could have known that terms such as "meditation," "Akashic records," "spiritual growth," "auras," "soul mates," and "holistic health" would become household words to millions?

INSULIN for DIABETES
Frederick Banting *discovers insulin as a treatment for Diabetes which came as a result of a two dream series.*

THEORY of RELATIVITY, (E=MC₂)
Albert Einstein *discovered this through a dream.*

DISCOVERY of THE MOLECULAR STRUCTURE OF THE ATOM
Niels Bohr *discovers the molecular structure of the atom, these are all secrets that God revealed through dreams and visions.*

THE SEWING MACHINE NEEDLE
Elias Howe, *inventor of the modern sewing machine, had been troubled by how to get the needle to work in his new invention. Having the eye at the base (as in handheld needles) was out of the question. Then, Popular Mechanics reported in 1905, he fell asleep:*

"One night he dreamed that he was building a sewing machine in a strange country for a savage king. The king had given him 24 hours to complete the machine and make it sew, but try as he would he could not make the needle work, and finally gave up in despair.

At sunrise he was taken out to be executed, and with the mechanical action of the mind in times of great crises he noted that the spears carried by the warriors were pierced near the head. Suddenly, he realized that here was the solution of the sewing machine needle. He begged for time—and while still begging, awoke. It was four o'clock. Hastily he dressed and went to his workshop—at nine o'clock the model of the needle with an eye at the point was finished

DNA
The shape and structure of DNA eluded scientists until 1953, when Dr. **James Watson** *had a dream that made him consider the double helix. According to Dr. Watson's alma mater, Indiana University, the dream was of two intertwined serpents with heads at opposite ends, though other accounts say the dream was of a double-sided staircase.*

Otto Loewi *(1873-1961), a German born physiologist, won the Nobel Prize for medicine in 1936 for his work on the chemical transmission of nerve impulses. In 1903, Loewi had the idea that there might be a chemical transmission of the nervous impulse rather than an electrical one, which was the common held belief, but he was at a loss on how to prove it. He let the idea slip to the back of his mind until 17 years later* **he had the following dream.** *According to Loewi:*

"The night before Easter Sunday of that year I awoke, turned on the light, and jotted down a few notes on a tiny slip of paper. Then I fell asleep again. It occurred to me at 6 o'clock in the morning that during the night I had written down something most important, but I was unable to decipher the scrawl. The next night, at 3 o'clock, the idea returned. It was the design of an experiment to determine whether or not the hypothesis of chemical transmission that I had uttered 17 years ago was correct.

Dr. Otto Loewi

I got up immediately, went to the laboratory, and performed a single experiment on a frog's heart according to the nocturnal design."
It took Loewi a decade to carry out a decisive series of tests to satisfy his critics, but ultimately the result of his initial dream induced experiment became the foundation for the theory of chemical transmission of the nervous impulse **and led to a Nobel Prize!**
Dr. Loewi noted: **"Most so called 'intuitive' discoveries are such associations made in the subconscious.**

"President Abraham Lincoln recounted the following dream to his wife just a few days prior to his assassination:
"About ten days ago, I retired very late. I had been up waiting for important dispatches from the front. I could not have been long in bed when I fell into a slumber, for I was weary.
I soon began to dream.

There seemed to be a death-like stillness about me. Then I heard subdued sobs, as if a number of people were weeping. I thought I left my bed and wandered downstairs. There the silence was broken by the same pitiful sobbing, but the mourners were invisible. I went from room to room; no living person was in sight, but the same mournful sounds of distress met me as I passed along. It was light in all the rooms; every object was familiar to me; but where were all the people who were grieving as if their hearts would break?

Currier & Ives print: The Assassination of President Lincoln Original - The Library of Congress

I was puzzled and alarmed. What could be the meaning of all this? Determined to find the cause of a state of things so mysterious and so shocking, I kept on until I arrived at the East Room, which I entered. There I met with a sickening surprise. Before me was a catafalque, on which rested a corpse wrapped in funeral vestments. Around it were stationed soldiers who were acting as guards; and there was a throng of people, some gazing mournfully upon the corpse whose face was covered, others weeping pitifully.

'Who is dead in the White House?' I demanded of one of the soldiers "The President" was his answer; "he was killed by an assassin!" Then came a loud burst of grief form the crowd, which awoke me from my dream."

Lincoln ascribed powerful meanings to his dreams. One of his recurring dreams in particular he considered foretelling and a sign of major events soon to occur. He had this dream the night before his assassination. On the morning of that lamentable day, President Lincoln was discussing matters of the war with General Grant during a cabinet meeting and believed that big news from General Sherman on the front would soon arrive. When Grant asked why he thought so, Lincoln responded:

"I had a dream last night; and ever since this war began I have had the same dream just before every event of great national importance. It portends some important event that will happen very soon."
His friend and law partner, Ward Hill Lamon, noted that Byron's "The Dream" was one of Lincoln's favorite poems and he often heard him repeat the following lines:
Sleep hath its own world,
A boundary between the things misnamed
Death and existence: Sleep hath its own world,
And a wide realm of wild reality,
And dreams in their development have breath,
And tears, and tortures, and the touch of joy;
They leave a weight upon our waking thoughts,
They take a weight from off waking toils,
They do divide our being;

Kekulé - Dreams of Molecules & Benzene Structure
Friedrich August Kekulé von Stradonitz is a remarkable figure in the history of chemistry, specifically organic chemistry.
Twice Kekulé had dreams that led to major discoveries!
Kekulé discovered the tetravalent nature of carbon, the formation of chemical/ organic "Structure Theory", but he did not make this breakthrough by experimentation alone. He had a dream! As he described in a speech given at the Deutsche Chemische Gesellschaft (German Chemical Society):

Kekulé in stamp form, celebrating his discovery of the Benzene structure... attributed to a dream!

"I fell into a reverie, and lo, the atoms were gamboling before my eyes! Whenever, hitherto, these diminutive beings had appeared to me, they had always been in motion; but up to that time, I had never been able to discern the nature of their motion. Now, however, I saw how, frequently, two smaller atoms united to form a pair; how a larger one embraced the two smaller ones; how still larger ones kept hold of three or even four of the smaller; whilst the whole kept whirling in a giddy dance. I saw how the larger ones formed a chain, dragging the smaller ones after them, but only at the ends of the chain. . . The cry of the conductor: "Clapham Road," awakened me from my dreaming; but I spent part of the night in putting on paper at least sketches of these dream forms. This was the origin of the Structural Theory."

Later, he had a dream that helped him discover that the Benzene molecule, unlike other known organic compounds, had a circular structure rather than a linear one... solving a problem that had been confounding chemists:

"...I was sitting writing on my textbook, but the work did not progress; my thoughts were elsewhere. I turned my chair to the fire and dozed. Again the atoms were gamboling before my eyes. This time the smaller groups kept modestly in the background. My mental eye, rendered more acute by the repeated visions of the kind, could now distinguish larger structures of manifold conformation; long rows sometimes more closely fitted together all twining and twisting in snake-like motion. But look! What was that? One of the snakes had seized hold of its own tail, and the form whirled mockingly before my eyes. As if by a flash of lightning I awoke; and this time also I spent the rest of the night in working out the consequences of the hypothesis."

The snake seizing it's own tail gave Kekulé the circular structure idea he needed to solve the Benzene problem!
Said an excited Kekulé to his colleagues, "Let us learn to dream!"

Madame C.J. Walker - From Dream to Millionaire

Madame C.J. Walker *(1867-1919) is cited by the Guinness Book of Records as the first female American self-made millionaire. She was also the first member of her family born free.*

Madame Walker founded and built a highly successful African-American cosmetic company that made her a millionaire many times over. Walker was suffering from a scalp infection that caused her to loose most of her hair in the 1890's. She began experimenting with patented medicines and hair-care products.

Then, she had a dream that solved her problems:
"He answered my prayer, for one night I had a dream, and in that dream a big, black man appeared to me and told me what to mix up in my hair. Some of the remedy was grown in Africa, but I sent for it, mixed it, put it on my scalp, and in a few weeks my hair was coming in faster than it had ever fallen out.

*Madame **Walker**honored on a US Postal Stamp.*

I tried it on my friends; it helped them. I made up my mind to begin to sell it."

Walker was an entrepreneur, philanthropist and social activist. She best sums up her rise from a childhood in the poor south to being the head of an international, multi-million dollar corporation in the following quote: "I am a woman who came from the cotton fields of the South. From there I was promoted to the washtub. From there I was promoted to the cook kitchen. And from there I promoted myself into the business of manufacturing hair goods and preparations....I have built my own factory on my own ground."

Sources: On Her Own Ground: the Life and Times of Madam C.J. Walker A'Lelia P. Bundles, 2001
MadamecjWalker.com

Mathematical Genius & Dreamer- Srinivasa Ramanujan

Srinivasa Ramanujan (1887-1920) was one of India's greatest mathematical geniuses. He made substantial contributions to analytical theory of numbers and worked on elliptical functions, continued fractions, and infinite series. In 1914, he was invited in to Cambridge University by the English mathematician GH Hardy who recognized his unconventional genius. He worked there for five years producing startling results and proved over 3,000 theorems in his lifetime.

According to Ramanujan, inspiration and insight for his work many times came to him in his dreams...

A Hindu goddess, named Namakkal, would appear and present mathematical formulae which he would verify after waking. Such dreams often repeated themselves and the connection with the dream world as a source for his work was constant throughout his life.

$$\frac{1}{\pi} = \frac{2\sqrt{2}}{9801} \sum_{k=0}^{\infty} \frac{(4k)!(1103 + 26390k)}{(k!)^4 396^{4k}}$$

Infinite series for π. Example of formulae Ramanujan developed that led to new directions of research.
Source: Wikipedia

Ramanujan describes one of his dreams of mathematical discovery:
"While asleep I had an unusual experience. There was a red screen formed by flowing blood as it were. I was observing it. Suddenly a hand began to write on the screen. I became all attention. That hand wrote a number of results in elliptic integrals. They stuck to my mind. As soon as I woke up, I committed them to writing..."

Subliminal Clues From Fossil Perceived In Dream

Louis Agassiz *(1807-1883) was a Swiss born naturalist, zoologist, geologist, and teacher who immigrated to the US in 1846. He trained and influenced a generation of American zoologists and paleontologists and is one of the founding fathers of the modern American scientific tradition*

*While Agassiz was working on his vast work "Poissons Fossiles" a list of all know fossil fish, he came across a specimen in a stone slab which he was, at first, unable to figure out. He hesitated to classify it and extract it since an incorrect approach could ruin the specimen. At that time,**Agassiz reports having a dream** three nights in a row in which he saw the fish in perfect original condition. The first two nights -- being unprepared -- he did not record his image.*

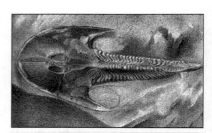

By the third night he was ready with pen and paper, and when the fish appeared again in the dream he drew it in the dark, still half asleep. The next day he looked at his drawing which had remarkably different features from the ones he had been working out, hastened to his laboratory and extracting the fossil realized it corresponded exactly to his dream.

Illustration of fossil fish from Les Poissons Fossiles, Louis Agassiz, 1843. Source: Strange Science

Agassiz' creative dream of the fossilized fish may have been induced by having perceived unconsciously a clue in the stone slab which he had ignored while awake.

His dream may have emphasized and drawn his attention to stimuli he had perceived subliminally while he was awake!

Source: Interview with Nikola Tesla, speaking of Agassiz, Tesla, The Modern Sorcerer Daniel Blair Stewart

George Washington Carver —
From the son of a slave to a great American scientist
The son of a slave, George Washington Carver was born in 1864 near the end of the Civil War. He was orphaned as a baby. When slavery was abolished the following year, his "owners," Moses and Susan Carver, raised George and his brother as their own.
He was taught to read and write, and later attended various schools and colleges, eventually earning a Master's degree from Iowa State University.

Show me secrets"
He would begin each day with prayer that God would reveal secrets to him about plants and vegetables. It is reported that once Carver prayed, "Mr. Creator, show me the secrets of your universe."

"Little man, you're not big enough to know the secrets of my universe, but I'll show you the secret of the peanut," was the reply.

George Washington Carver *ca. 1910*
His prayer and heaven's response launched him into a lifetime of discovery.
In 1941, Time magazine called Carver a "Black Leonardo," a reference to the Italian Renaissance man, Leonardo da Vinci.
Giving himself to the lowly peanut, he identified several hundred elements in its seed and shell.
As he put the elements together again in different forms, he uncovered over 300 uses for the peanut including various kinds of foods, oil, paint, ink, soap, shampoo, facial cream, plastics, and many other products.
But there is a God in heaven who reveals secrets ... (Daniel 2:28)
Later Carver lifted the sweet potato saying, "Show me its secrets."
Again, fresh discoveries and opportunities flowed through his work – over 115 products were developed from the sweet potato including flour, starch, and synthetic rubber.

For more books or request you can contact us via Amazon.com, also @ Facebook.com.

DREAMS & VISIONS GROUPS on Facebook.com
Dreams , Visions, and Prayer

Also www.facebook.com/groups/knightsunite